How to Be a Christian Woman

(when you still want to slap people)

Workbook Devotional & Guided Journal

An 8-Week Faith Journey

(with 12 days of bonus sass!)

by Kimberly Billings

FAVOR DEI
PRESS
NEW YORK

How to Be a Christian Woman
(when you still want to slap people)
Second Edition

Library of Congress Control Number: 2025911242

Cover Designer: Kimberly Billings

Book Interior Designer: Bianca Jones

ISBN: 979-8-218-68176-0

Printed in United States of America

Table of Contents

Week 3: Patchwork & Grace — Healing and Restoration

Memory Verse: 2 Corinthians 12:9 — 'My grace is sufficient for you, for my power is made perfect in weakness.'

Week 4: Faith in the Wild — Living it Out in Everyday Chaos

Memory Verse: 1 Thessalonians 5:16-18 — 'Rejoice always, pray continually, give thanks in all circumstances...'

- Day 2 — God Bless You (No, really!)

- Day 3 — Find a Penny, Preach a Prayer

- Day 4 — Conversations with God

- Day 5 — Putting the God in Godson

- Day 6 — What's Your Lenten Promise?

- Day 7 — Praise God That I Bear That Name

Week 5: Mirror, Mirror — Reflection and Wisdom

Memory Verse: James 1:5 — 'If any of you lacks wisdom, you should ask God... and it will be given to you.'

- Day 1 — Pop Quiz

- Day 2 — Double Standard?

- Day 3 — A Nice Way to End a Great Week...

- Day 4 — Fashion Fads, Flying Boxers...

- Day 5 — 10 Random Facts About Me

- Day 6 — Things That Make Me Happy

- Day 7 — Evidence...

Week 6: Still Standing — God's Faithfulness in Every Season

Memory Verse: Isaiah 40:31 — 'But those who hope in the Lord will renew their strength...'

- Day 1 — Take Not Thy Holy Spirit from Me
- Day 2 — Cast Me Not Away
- Day 3 — Renew My Spirit
- Day 4 — Restore My Joy
- Day 5 — Uphold Me with Thy Free Spirit
- Day 6 — Peace Be with You
- Day 7 — How Great Thou Art

Week 7: Called, Not Comfortable — Purpose, Boldness & Kingdom Work

Memory Verse: Ephesians 2:10 — 'For we are God's handiwork, created in Christ Jesus to do good works...'

- Day 1 — Reasons and Seasons
- Day 2 — Faith, Hope and Love
- Day 3 — Faith, Hope and Love, Part 2
- Day 4 — Life... it's Past, Present, Future... Forever
- Day 5 — Divine Intervention
- Day 6 — Favor
- Day 7 — The Best Gift

Week 8: Cue the Confetti — Joy, Victory & Forward Momentum

Memory Verse: Philippians 1:6 — 'He who began a good work in you will carry it on to completion...'

Dedication

Dedicated to my God-given husband, Eric, to my beautiful, amazing children (ALL of them: bio, step, God, and students), to all of my friends and family who have supported, encouraged, and helped to grow my faith, and most importantly, to Our Lord and Savior Jesus Christ, for His constant outpouring of grace and mercy, without which I would have nothing to write, and I would remain lost.

Introduction

Welcome, sister. Whether you're barely hanging on by a thread or just needing a holy reset, this workbook is your spiritual pit stop. Over the next 8 weeks, we'll walk through real struggles, deep grace, and honest to-goodness transformation — all with a little sass and a whole lot of Jesus.

Each week focuses on a different theme, grounded in truth, guided by Scripture, and filled with journaling prompts, prayers, and chapter-based reflections. Use this journal however you need: daily, weekly, in your messy kitchen, or your quiet morning spot. Just show up — because God always does.

Let's do this. Coffee in hand, Bible open, and heart ready.

Love,

Kim

Prologue

I think this book is more for me than it is for anyone else. It took me years to accumulate all the chapters. Some of the messages have evolved because, well, I have evolved. For instance, I used to reference the NIV, but this book only cites the ESV Bible. Other than that, I don't want to say I've "changed" because I still feel like I'm me, I'm just a better version of me. Make sense? Don't answer that. Even if it doesn't to you, I'm sticking by it.

When I write, I tend to write as though I am speaking to a friend, so if I offend, maybe pass this book along to someone who can handle musings of my level of snarky, sassy, and slightly-inappropriate-at times. I will tell you this: I was rather restrained and "sweet". Yeah, I be like that. (Except for like THAT; I'm a huge grammar geek, but I thought saying "I be like that" is cute) Let it go. Moving on.

Ok, let me give a little background on me to get you started. Born of a Lutheran mom and Roman Catholic (non-practicing, but now faithful Lutheran) dad. Mom was born and raised Lutheran of a mother and grandmother who were also active in their Lutheran churches in Queens. I attended Sunday School as soon as I was old enough (4 maybe?) and kept regular attendance through grade 6, after which I did my 2-year stint in confirmation classes. First Holy Communion and Confirmation celebrated a week apart in spring of my 8th grade year 1984). I was trained as an acolyte by my then pastor, Pastor John Collier. I guess I did right by him because I was regularly called to fill in for no-shows (good man, tough cookie). Everything from right to left on the right side, left to right on the left side, bottom to top toward the cross, bow in reverence at the cross each time you pass in front of it. To be sure, a quick glance to Pastor for approval and I was in the clear. My type-A self-loved the particulars, the rules, and the meanings behind all of them. This definitely helped me be accurate and remain focused. That was a good set up for when I served on Altar Guild years later. I loved that job, too.

Throughout childhood and through to today, music has been pretty much one of my most favorite things. My dad is a musician, and I grew up hearing him practice every day. It was just natural that I study an instrument, and it ended up being violin. I started in third grade, and I stuck with it through senior year in high school, even achieving first chair and being "president" (which meant nothing, but made me feel good, nonetheless). I also sang from the moment I could talk - Dad made sure of that. Somewhere there's a cassette with my two-year-old voice singing Twinkle Twinkle. I kept that up (yes, I ventured to more difficult pieces of music) throughout all of my school years in various choirs, in the adult choir at church, then lots of singing in adulthood (fronted a band, did some karaoke, I even sang with Dad and his bandmate). What prompted this whole paragraph?

Oh, I guess to let you know more about me. Continue, please.

Anyway, this book is going to let you in... like, *really* into my life. Everything from cover to cover are 100% my life experiences.

No one has seen what I've seen, done what I've done, or been where I've been. D@mn, I just made my life sound awful! It really hasn't been! I've been quite blessed and, from those times when I've struggled, I'm able to look back and see the gift God has given me by allowing certain things to happen (remember Job? Dude had FAITH.)

I've been writing this for, well, years. Yeah. I write, I lose it, I write more. I lose it again. Writer's block is no joke, friends. My faith has done some big evolving over the years, but then again, shouldn't it? God allowed me to travel through some bigtime rough patches in the 2000s and early 2010s. He also gave me the most incredible gift for my continued (though, at times, strained, don't get me wrong) faith in His plan: Eric, a man of faith with whom I can share my life.

How'd we meet? Sharing the peace across the center aisle at church (he, a left-side-of-the-church Lutheran, I, a forever right-side-girl... Lutherans, you feel me? I know you do.)

How'd it start? Jimmy, our dear friend and the head elder at church, planted a seed in both our brains and before you knew it, one fateful Friday night in September, Eric bought me dinner. (Between you and me, I think that night he realized I was the one; he fed me for under $5 at Taco Bell and I'm pretty sure baseball was involved.)

We got married on August 5, 2017, and again on August 6, 2017. Renewed our vows along with the whole congregation in a sweet little Valentine's Day worship service in February 2018. Dude must REALLY love me to marry me 3x. That will most likely inspire a second book.

Eric has guided me along my journey in faith in some way every day. I don't tell him nearly enough how important he is to me, what a blessing he is, and how much I love him. So, in large part he is responsible for this book to actually get off the ground.

In 2 years and 1 month I will retire from my life-long career as a public-school teacher. It's time, and, although I've greatly enjoyed these past 33+ years so far, things are quite different now in education than they were in 1992. I am looking forward to leaving the secular teaching world in the rearview mirror and embarking on deepening my faith and seeking Him wholeheartedly like never before. And you get to come along for the ride!

We summer in our beloved Ocean Grove, where my spiritual life changed forever in 2015 with my first visit. Eric has been going to OG his entire life, and before him, his mom and grandparents. We both serve in the ministry there; I, as a proud alto in the Auditorium Choir, an active member of the Ladies Auxiliary, and co-chair of the Summer Marketplace, Eric as an Auditorium Usher and a "voluntold" (Hilary gets credit for that word - basically, whatever I'm involved in, he automatically gets to help). Anyway, OG is a truly blessed place, and I encourage all of you to go visit.

Although the church that is kind of "home base" for Auditorium Worship and Beach Church is Methodist, we pray, sing, and hear a message from people of various faiths. None of what we do there contradicts or counters our Lutheran beliefs but allows us to serve God while we're not at our home church. This is cool because, inevitably, it sparks some deep, theological conversation and, dare I say, educated banter among us neighbors. I don't know if that's how I should explain it. Bottom line: lifelong Lutherans, Eric and Kim, get to impart LCMS Lutheranism to everyone (and proudly)!

Our service at our home church is equally as committed. Actually, more so due to the fact that we're there year-round.

Eric is a Communion Steward and serves weekly at the community meal served at our church on Sundays. I was a member of the choir (which sadly stopped) and I proudly read the epistle every couple of weeks. I have held MANY different Council positions but currently am back to doing my favorite one: Council Secretary. In any capacity, I'm proud to serve. I also have known for quite some time now that I am called to do more.

For several years I have had this idea taking up space in my head that I'd like to be a deacon. I have always wanted to serve in a bigger capacity somehow, but I believe that women have a specific/restricted set of roles in which they are able to serve within the church. Most recently, I have taken on reviving Emanuel's LWML group! As the head of our group, I have been able to meet inspiring members from other churches, reconnect with amazing women and old friends across our district who I've known for years. Still, something has been stirring inside me. Yup. There has to be more.

Natalie, Pastor's wife, and I were having dinner after a day of thrifting when I casually mentioned the thought of being a deacon. Natalie nearly spit out her pancakes and jumped out of our iHop booth. "OMGSH PLEASE, YES! That would be amazing and will help Steven so much!" so, I prayed on it and consequently checked into it. LCMS has an INCREDIBLE Deaconess program at the seminary that, no doubt, would be a truly amazing academic, spiritual, and theological journey, but let's face it, I'm 55 and not going back into the classroom. I can't even remember what I ate for dinner last night, ain't no way I can take post-grad classes like that.

However, my new friend, Deaconess Raquel Rojas, has my undying and utmost admiration for being a graduate of that program. There is another route, I discovered. A Lay Deacon is one that is less of a ministry role, not an ordained position or anything, but would allow me, under Pastor's guidance and leadership, to comfort others, pray with the sick and shut in, and greatly assist the pastor in various capacities. It's a two-year program run by our district and Pastor Steve very eagerly supported my decision to apply. I am proud to announce that, in March, I was accepted as an Atlantic District Lay Deacon Candidate of the Class of 2027. I will "graduate" the very month I will retire from my secular job!

God, You knew all along, didn't You? Oh, yeah, You did!

God, You knew I was gonna write a book, didn't You? Sure, You did!

I'm taking this a step further and this book will have a companion workbook that can be used as a personal devotional/study guide or as a group study. I pray this is a blessing for you all and that, over time, it grows not only your faith, but mine as well.

Peace,

Kim

Week 1

Wake Up, Sister - Self-Awareness and Honesty

This week is all about cracking open the hard shell of denial and getting real with yourself and with God. No more pretending everything's fine when it's not. We're flipping the light switch on the dark corners of our soul and asking God to show us the mess — not so we can wallow in it, but so He can start the cleanup. Get ready to feel a little exposed, a little convicted, and a lot loved.

Guided Prayer to Start the Week

Father, awaken my spirit. Help me to see what You see when You look at me. Strip away the filters of shame, comparison, and pride. Let me be brave enough to face the truth about myself — and bold enough to make any changes I should.

Day 1 — In the Beginning

I have known for a while that I craved a personal space where I could express myself (by writing) my ideas, my hopes, etc. I have a lot to say (those who know me personally are nodding) and should I become a better version of myself in the future, I'll have a place to see my progress in the journey. This yearning, I believe, echoes the sentiment in Psalm 19:14:

> *"Let the words of my mouth and the meditation of my hear the acceptable in your sight, O Lord, my rock and my redeemer."*

I started with a blog. I started it several years ago when I had a gazillion things in my head that needed to come out. Sometimes I wake up with an idea. Sometimes the ideas come to me as I'm about to fall asleep. Sometimes I'm driving or teaching or sitting in church when an idea hits; I often lose those ideas, although now I try to use talk-to-text to record them in the notes app on my phone. This has led me to realize that I have a different purpose. I do, according to God, have a calling! I sense a stirring within me, a divine nudge toward something more, just as the Apostle Paul wrote in Romans 11:29,

> *"For the gifts and the calling of God are irrevocable,"*

For as long as I remember, my Christian faith has been a huge part of who I am. Admittedly, I do not always exhibit the most Christian-like behaviors, speak kind words, or even act kindly. I sin.

I'm REALLY good at it, too. At this point in my life (mid-50s as I write this) I find myself on a constant mission to recognize my sin and reconcile myself with God. It's a daily mission, an all-day mission, an I'm-never-gonna-know-all-my-sins mission. I'm a work-in progress and I will be one until the Lord takes me Home. It is a comfort to remember the words of 1 John 1:8:

> "If we say we have no sin, we deceive ourselves, and the truth is not in us."

This truth, as Martin Luther so powerfully preached, drives us to the foot of the cross, seeking God's unending grace.

There was a brief time in my 20s when I didn't attend church regularly (shocker - there are stories and I am VERY glad social media was not a thing back then) . I was living in Rhode Island at the time and the only Lutheran church I could find was part of a synod of which I was not a member, nor a fan. That church's views were far more progressive than what I was comfortable with and, although I somewhat admired the fact that a woman played an active role in the worship service, something didn't sit right.

To this day I remain rather hard-wired in my thinking that my pastor should be a man. He is the shepherd of a flock, like Jesus was...no, is. My shepherd will always have to be a man. Call me old-fashioned all you want, I just think men are better in leadership roles (GASP - did I actually just type that? That's it, I'm about to be "canceled" as is custom nowadays). God made MAN first, in His image, and the leaders of the early church stemming from the disciples were men. I truly believe God intends only men to be the heads of the church.

However, something always pulled me towards wanting to do more and be more in my faith-life. Upon returning to live in NY, I dove headfirst into Bible study, devotions, church activities, teaching Sunday School, VBS, singing in the choir, I have even held a few Council positions. I am fascinated by Greek and Hebrew words, phrases, and translations.

I always want to learn more. The Bible became less scary and more of a "life's instruction book". The more I learn, the more I want to make it a part of my calling and my purpose. I accept God's call to learn as much as I can, to share what I know, to witness and edify His name. This resonates deeply with my desire to understand and share God's Word:

> *"Do your best to present yourself to God as one approved, a worker who has no need to be ashamed, rightly handling the word of truth."* 2 Timothy 2:15

Sounds like I had it all figured out, right? Hahahaha!! Oh, please, I told you earlier, I'm what you might call a "professional sinner". My sass mouth still gets me into trouble, earns me some enemies, and my taste in music is constantly evolving toward more and more, how should I put this, "creative and colorful" lyrics. Yet, even in my daily (all-day) struggles, I can find solace in Romans 8:1: "There is therefore now no condemnation for those who are in Christ Jesus."

This powerful declaration reminds us that God's grace covers our imperfections, as I am saved "by grace, through faith" (Ephesians 2:8). What about my career? The thing I do for hours every day that helps me pay my bills.

My daytime career as a teacher is a part of me, yes. As I write this, I am in my 33rd year of teaching and I have a mere 2 years until I retire. However, my career (profession) no longer defines me. Although it continues to be a fun, challenging, and truly fulfilling way to pass my days (and pay the aforementioned bills), I am a mother, too. Motherhood is a full-time job that does define a huge part of my identity, but my first calling, being a Christian, helps me to be the best mother and teacher I can be.

I have recently come to realize that, for me, being a teacher is the career of a lifetime, being a mother is the role of a lifetime, but being a Christian is the call of a lifetime. I am called to be each of these, but my call to faith will serve to be the most rewarding of all.

> *"Search me, God, and know my heart; test me and know my anxious thoughts."* Psalm 139:23

Today I'm Feeling:

_____

Today's Struggle:

_____

Small Victory Today:

_____

Where I Saw God Today:

_____

Prayer for Today:

_____

_____

_____

_____

_____

_____

Reflect: What needs a fresh start in me today?

_____

_____

_____

_____

Chapter Reflection: How did my first day with this study set the tone for what I'm hoping to learn?

_____

_____

_____

_____

_____

Journal

_____

_____

_____

_____

_____

_____

_____

_____

_____

Doodle space:

Day 2 — Lean not

Trust in the Lord with all your heart, and do not lean on your own understanding. in all your ways acknowledge him, and he will make straight your paths. (Proverbs 3:5-6)

I have a really rough time trusting. I don't claim to have lived some crazy life that led me to this, but I'm sure some of my experiences have shaped my mistrust in MAN (not any particular man, just MAN, like human) . So, why is it difficult for me to trust God?

Sinful being that I am, I constantly want to do things MY WAY. I am a classic overthinker, compulsive and impulsive. I see something I'd like to have; I obsess over it until I have it. If I have an idea about how something should be done, I will argue against deviating from it or pout if I lose. This is a HUGE vice that I have to fight against.

Fight? No, pray about. You see, my focus is not on God when I'm acting that way. Only God knows what's best and what will inevitably happen. I have to learn to trust in His plan.

So, lately, as I've found myself battling some personal demons, God is sending me messages through devotions I read, verses on images within Bible and devotion apps, and various ways embedded in worship services. Start with a web search for "Bible verses about____" and click on the Images tab...

> *"Trust in the Lord with all your heart and lean not on your own understanding."* Proverbs 3:5

Today I'm Feeling:

_____

Today's Struggle:

_____

Small Victory Today:

_____

Where I Saw God Today:

_____

Prayer for Today:

_____

_____

_____

_____

_____

Reflect: Where am I leaning on my own understanding
instead of trusting God?

_____

_____

_____

_____

_____

Chapter Reflection: What area of life do I need to hand over to God even though it's hard?

_____

_____

_____

_____

_____

Journal

_____

_____

_____

_____

_____

_____

_____

Doodle space:

Day 3 — Who's Your Daddy?

I need constant refocusing prompts regarding my faith. My mind (you ladies can sympathize) is like having 25 tabs open all at once on a web browser. The most important tab, the one that should eliminate all the others, is my God tab. But I keep opening and searching, like the sinful, unworthy being I am. Yet, I named the URL for the blog I used to have (By Grace Through Faith), "Favor Dei" which allows me to refocus and start anew every single time I realize my tabs are out of control.

This book is my latest creation to help grow my faith and improve my ministry. My focus MUST be my Father in heaven ALL.THE.TIME. I read in my devotions almost every day that He is in control of EVERYTHING. So, why worry or be anxious about anything? Sounds easy enough, though quite hard to do.

> *He is not afraid of bad news; his heart is firm, trusting in the Lord.* Psalm 112:7

When we worry, are anxious, have doubts, or are scared, those things become our god! We're focused on everything BUT the only One who can help us, guide us, and calm us. We need only to worship the one true God, our Heavenly Father and Creator.

So, who's your daddy? Call on Him, and guess what? He's happy you're back - everyday! No questions, no conditions, nothing but favor.

Be blessed as you read... Peace

"The Spirit you received brought about your adoption to sonship. And by him we cry, 'Abba, Father.'" Romans 8:15

Today I'm Feeling:

_____

Today's Struggle:

_____

Small Victory Today:

_____

Where I Saw God Today:

_____

Prayer for Today:

_____

_____

_____

_____

_____

Reflect: What keeps me from fully embracing God as my Father?

_____

_____

_____

_____

_____

Chapter Reflection: What would change if I lived today like I belonged completely to God?

_____

_____

_____

_____

Journal

_____

_____

_____

_____

_____

_____

_____

_____

_____

_____

_____

Doodle space:

Day 4 — Life as a Type-A

What's the big deal? Don't we all have our little quirks and routines that keep our lives in order? I mean, who doesn't reconcile their grocery receipts against their purchases? And let's be real—if you stray from your daily routine, doesn't it feel like the universe has flipped upside down?

So, why not embrace it?! BECAUSE I WILL LOSE MY MIND! If that happens, I can't promise I'll be very Christian in my reaction. Life can be a struggle sometimes. I just can't let go of control over certain things.

Cleaning the bathroom? My territory. Washing clothes? Sure, but folding? H*ll no, I'll just live out of my "clean hamper" and buy new underwear if I have to. Bagging my groceries? That's a sacred art that only I can master.

Follow me here:

So, there's this new grocery store that opened nearby. My friend, who's been raving about it, took me along. Apparently, they have insanely low prices. But first, I had to wrap my brain around a few rules. First, bring my own bags. That's easy, I live in NY, I hoard reusable bags and totes. I have a whole stash in my car for just such a moment.

Second, to get a shopping cart, you have to stick a quarter into a lock release (really weird, but ok). Lastly, when you check out, the CASHIER throws (ok, maybe "throws" is a little harsh, but they definitely do not "place gently") your items into another cart (and then you get to play "bag your own groceries" at a long table). Could I manage that? I asked myself? I always load the belt myself, placing the items in the order in which they will be bagged, and then, how they are separated and stored in the house. Doesn't everyone? Anyway, I cautiously agreed to go and we were off.

We marched in, and from the get-go, I was impressed. No flashy displays, just pallets of what LOOKED like my favorite foods. The packaging looks SIMILAR to the brand name version and they're about a third of the price! I loaded up my cart, feeling like a grocery warrior.

However, when I got to the checkout, the cashier started ringing up my items like she was in a race. I tried to keep up, but it was like a game of Grocery Tetris.

"Wait! No! You can't stack the cans and veggies like that! Don't put that on top of the —"

Crap! Panic mode activated.

Oh, the attitude I caught from the cashier when I raged! I wanted to scream, but instead, I breathed deeply, muttered and paid, then rolled my cart to the long table. I packed each item into my bags with my normal precision and care. "A place for everything and everything in its place!" I told myself. I survived, barely, muttering some choice words, loaded the bags into my trunk, and of course, I made sure to reclaim my quarter!

Let's be real: we all have our delightful little quirks that make us who we are. You know that moment when you walk into a public restroom (like at the mall) and see water and soap smeared all over the sink? Yep, I'm that person who wipes it clean like I'm auditioning for a cleaning commercial. And if you need to change the toilet paper roll in my bathroom? Just remember: the paper goes OVER, okay?

Here's the kicker: as much as I love my routines, I'm reminded of

> *"Trust in the Lord with all your heart, and do not lean on your own understanding; in all your ways acknowledge Him, and He will make straight your paths."* Proverbs 3:5-6

Maybe, just maybe, I need to loosen my grip a little and remember that God's in control, not me!

So, love me, love my quirks, and let's all learn to let go a bit. After all, life's too short to sweat the small stuff—especially when there's grocery shopping to do! Sure glad I beat that old lady to the good parking spot...

LOL jk

> *"Be still and know that I am God."* Psalm 46:10

Today I'm Feeling:

_____

Today's Struggle:

_____

Small Victory Today:

_____

Where I Saw God Today:

_____

Prayer for Today:

_____

_____

_____

_____

_____

Reflect: Where am I trying to control what God is already managing?

_____

_____

_____

_____

_____

Chapter Reflection: What does "being still" look like in my Type-A reality?

_____

_____

_____

_____

_____

Journal

_____

_____

_____

_____

_____

_____

_____

_____

Doodle space:

Day 5 — The War on Christmas?

This is a little trick my former Pastor taught us one year... how to keep Christ in XMAS by writing Rho (P) in the center of the "X"... this is translated as ₽ a common Christian symbol meaning "Christ."

I was at home sick for a couple of days and much of the time I spent watching the news. The beginning of December is chock-full of references to Christmas, shopping, the economy, and the annual "War on Christmas". There is a whole lot to think about (which I have). So, I figured I'd do a little research and write down some thoughts on this.

Sitting here on the couch, I find myself often looking at the Christmas decorations that adorn my house: the tree, the Santas (I'm a big fan), the Nativity, the wreaths, the red and green. What is the origin of all these things that are tradition during Christmas? My research shocked me. I was a bit surprised by what I discovered (cue tragic music). However, (cue inspiring music), I soon realized that the last place I looked should have been the first.

Apparently, Christmas indeed was loosely connected to a pagan celebration: Saturnalia. There were parties, gift-giving, even good-will toward men. It was only a few centuries ago that these pagan rituals began to be dropped from its Saturnalia connection to adhere more toward the Christian celebration of Christ's birth. However, some cultures forbade the celebration of Christmas (the Puritans for example) for a long time.

Okay, so that whole Christmas tree, holly, mistletoe, and even those cute gingerbread men we devour? Turns out, sometimes the things we associate with Christian celebrations have some pagan roots, in this case, going way back to the Romans and their party for the sun god, Saturn.

Do a quick search – some of it is kinda creepy when you look at it through our Jesus-tinted glasses. Now, the Bible never actually tells us to throw a birthday bash for Jesus on December 25th. It wasn't until a few centuries after He was born that the early church started officially celebrating it around that time. Some Christians are really tied to having it all exactly as it's written, no wiggle room. They see all these traditions as just "man-made stuff" that can take away from what God really intends. I get where they're coming from, that whole "Scriptura Sola" thing is VERY important to us Lutherans.

However, here's where I kinda go "hold up." For us, it's not like if it's not in the Bible, it's automatically evil. Luther was rather on board with as long as we're not, you know, sacrificing goats to a Christmas tree (pretty sure we're good there!), these traditions can be ways we show our joy and celebrate Jesus' birth in our own cultural way. The big thing is making sure we don't lose sight of why we're doing all this – it's all about Jesus, not some ancient Roman rave.

Martin Luther was all about keeping Christmas Christ-centered—even while enjoying the fun stuff like carols, trees, and gifts. To him, the real heart of the season was the birth of the greatest gift we've ever received: Jesus Christ, God's own Son. Luther wanted the nativity scene and the infant Jesus to be front and center—nothing else compared.

So, I did a little deep dive (geeked out on Lutheran history) to see how our brother Martin viewed Christmas. Here's what I found out:

- All About the Incarnation: Luther believed Christmas should focus on the miracle of God becoming human in Jesus. He often preached about "the Word became flesh and made His dwelling among us," and he didn't want people to lose sight of how huge that is.
- Gifts with a Gospel Twist: For Luther, giving gifts—especially to children—was a perfect chance to teach about the free gift of grace and salvation we receive through Jesus. That's the real present under the tree.
- Sing It Loud: Luther was big on Christmas carols. He believed they helped capture the joy and awe of Christ's birth in a way that sermons sometimes couldn't.
- Trees and Candles: While Luther might not have "invented" the Christmas tree, stories about him using candles on evergreen branches point to his love of nature and light—symbolizing Christ, the Light of the world.
- Christkind (Christ Child): Instead of the jolly man in red, Luther encouraged celebrating the Christ Child as the true giver of gifts. It's His birthday, after all.
- Worship is a Must: Luther made it clear—go to church on Christmas. Worship, hear the Word, and rejoice in what God has done. That's what the holiday is really about.
- Look Inward Too: He also encouraged taking time for personal reflection—what does the Incarnation mean for you? How does Christ's coming change your life?

Traditions? Sure—With the Right Focus: Luther didn't totally dismiss all the warm-and-fuzzy traditions. Family time, music, even festive customs were fine—as long as they kept the focus on Jesus, the Savior of the world.

One more quote to solidify my point. Martin Luther, the leader of the Reformation, only discarded those teachings and practices that contradicted the Gospel and Scripture. He said,

> *"We do not condemn the doctrines of men just because they are the doctrines of men, for we would gladly put up with them. But we condemn them because they are contrary to the gospel and the Scriptures. While the Scriptures liberate consciences and forbid that they be taken captive by the doctrines of men, these doctrines of men captivate the conscience anyhow (A Reply to the Texts, LW 35:153; WA 10II:91.)*

Therefore, I will continue to celebrate my Savior's birth. I will continue to joyfully wish folks "Merry Christmas". I will always decorate with red and green, a tree, lights, Santa (I love Santa), and my Nativity scene (my Fisher Price© one is my favorite). I will give gifts to my loved ones and I will feast on high calorie treats at Christmas parties. I will share the Christmas story with anyone, anywhere (except for work, I might get fired... sad) and all the while keeping the TRUE meaning of Christmas: a child was born to save me... and YOU!

> *"The Word became flesh and made his dwelling among us."* John 1:14

Today I'm Feeling:

_____

Today's Struggle:

_____

Small Victory Today:

_____

Where I Saw God Today:

_____

Prayer for Today:

_____

_____

_____

_____

Reflect: Have I been focused on the wrong "wars"?

_____

_____

_____

Chapter Reflection: How can I keep Christ at the center in a culture full of distractions?

_____

_____

_____

_____

_____

Journal

_____

_____

_____

_____

_____

_____

_____

_____

_____

Doodle space:

Day 6 — Sticks and Stones

"Sticks and stones may break my bones, but words will never hurt me." Whoever created this sentence was probably never teased but was the teaser.

Today my daughter came home in tears; several boys teased her about liking another boy, although she insisted to them that it wasn't true and that they are just friends. They drove her to the point of yelling, which she doesn't do, and she burst into tears. She opened up to me in the car; I saw immediately that she was upset and said, "Talk to me. What happened?"

It was as though I was transported by time machine to 1970-something when being teased was almost a daily occurrence for me. Getting teased hurts so badly. I wasn't teased about liking a boy, like my daughter was, I was teased about my weight. However, back in the 70's, weight-consciousness and exercise to keep oneself fit wasn't as common a topic. So, while it hurt being teased for being "chubby," I didn't know how to change who I was to stop the torture. Drinking Tab and starving myself was not going to work for me.

My daughter is another story. She is thin. I guess I thought I was out of the woods from hearing about kids teasing her. I would do anything to trade places with her and take away the hurt. Of course, being 40 (if you believe I'm 40 I have a bridge to sell you), I told her the only advice I could think of: "Don't let them see that it bothers you."

That's almost as bad as the sticks and stones thing...

I told her that I was so sorry for what happened and that it hurts me, too, to know that she is going through this. I wish there was a clear answer as to why kids tease and how to stop it, but there isn't. Kids can be hurtful and thoughtless. I try to raise my girls to be mindful of others' feelings, as do most parents (I hope), but when they are on the receiving end, how do I cope? How do I help my girls cope?

> *"There is one whose rash words are like sword thrusts, but the tongue of the wise brings healing."* Proverbs 12:18

I strive to raise my girls to be kind and considerate, like most good parents aim for, but it's tough when they're on the receiving end. So, what do I do? I remind them to be strong, to lean on their faith, and that they are loved. After all, Romans 8:37 tells us, *"...in all these things, we are more than conquerors through him who loved us."*

I just say, "Be strong, my girls, be strong... I love you."

> *"The tongue has the power of life and death."* Proverbs 18:21

Today I'm Feeling:

_____

Today's Struggle:

_____

Small Victory Today:

_____

Where I Saw God Today:

_____

Prayer for Today:

_____

_____

_____

_____

_____

Reflect: What words have stuck with me — for better or worse?

_____

_____

_____

_____

Chapter Reflection: How do my words reflect the state of my heart?

_____

_____

_____

_____

_____

Journal

_____

_____

_____

_____

_____

_____

_____

_____

Doodle space:

Day 7 — mean

"There is one whose rash words are like sword thrusts, but the tongue of the wise brings healing." Proverbs 12:18

The title is intentionally written in lower-case to reflect the small-mindedness of those who bully. Ever since I did a ton of research on cyberbullying years ago, I have thought a lot about several kids who were horribly cruel to me and to other kids when we were growing up. There are a few names and faces in my memory that I will never forget. Their immature, cutting comments are imprinted on my brain, as I'm sure others have similar memories that haunt them. I was then reminded of a few names and faces of those I treated with disrespect and meanness.

"I tell you, on the day of judgment people will give account for every careless word they speak" Matthew 12:36

Ever hear the song by Taylor Swift called "Mean." It was the inspiration for this post. Here is the first verse:

You, with your words like knives
And swords and weapons that you use against me
You, have knocked me off my feet again
Got me feeling like a nothing
You, with your voice like nails on a chalkboard
Calling me out when I'm wounded
You, picking on the weaker man
Well, you can take me down
With just one single blow

I actually have to disagree about the "weaker man" line. I believe (as an adult) that the bully is the weaker man. Kids who pick on others are insecure about themselves; in order to empower themselves, they demean others.

They are so hurting inside that they want to hurt others to make themselves feel better. Try telling that to the kid who is a little chubby, doesn't have the most stylish clothing, hairstyle or the best skin. That kid has enough issues; he doesn't need someone pointing out what makes him different. I think the weaker one (the bully) has even more issues. Those who bully may seem strong in the moment, but God sees everything — even the "small" hurts — and He will hold people accountable.

Here is the next verse from Taylor Swift's song:

You, with your switching sides
And your walk-by lies
And your humiliation
You have pointed out my flaws again
As if I don't already see them
I walk with my head down
Trying to block you out
Cause I'll never impress you
I just want to feel okay again
I'll bet you got pushed around
Somebody made you cold
But the cycle ends right now
Cause you can't lead me down that road
And you don't know what you don't know

When I wrote the chapter "Sticks and Stones" that was generally about teasing, but the same can be said for bullying. It's been said, "if a boy teases a girl, he must like her." Sometimes I think that's true, sometimes I think he is just a bully, showing how weak and insecure he is. As a parent, I hate the thought of anyone saying something mean to my children or of my children saying something mean to someone else.

Kids who are teased or bullied NEVER forget the words that cut so deep. Those words will remain with them forever and mold them into who they become as adults. We need to help all children learn to cope with this; it can be very damaging to their future relationships. My girls have a Christian education to back up what I try to teach them at home about being kind, thoughtful, respectful and loving to one another. We, as parents, grandparents, older siblings and adults in general, have a moral obligation to teach all children how to treat others this way.

The cycle of cruelty stops when someone chooses to break it by being better, not bitter. It doesn't matter if someone is Christian, Jewish, Muslim or atheist... the underlying theme remains the same: treat others as you want to be treated and love one another. Kindness is a universal truth. Jesus said the same.

> *"So, whatever you wish that others would do to you, do also to them, for this is the Law and the Prophets."*
> Matthew 7:12

Even when people hurt us, deep love and compassion (rooted in Christ) can bring restoration — to them and to us.

"Do not be overcome by evil but overcome evil with good." Romans 12:21

"Above all, keep loving one another earnestly, since love covers a multitude of sins." 1 Peter 4:8

"Be kind and compassionate to one another, forgiving each other, just as in Christ God forgave you." Ephesians 4:32

Today I'm Feeling:

_____

Today's Struggle:

_____

Small Victory Today:

_____

Where I Saw God Today:

_____

Prayer for Today:

_____

_____

_____

_____

_____

Reflect: Who do I need to be kinder to today — including myself?

_____

_____

_____

_____

_____

Chapter Reflection: When have I been "mean," and how is God inviting me to grow in grace?

_____

_____

_____

_____

_____

Journal

_____

_____

_____

_____

_____

_____

_____

_____

_____

_____

Doodle space:

End-of-Week Reflection

What did I discover about myself this week?

_____

_____

_____

_____

_____

Where did God meet me in my honesty?

_____

_____

_____

_____

_____

What do I want to carry forward into next week?

_____

_____

_____

_____

_____

Biggest Growth Moment:

_____

_____

_____

_____

_____

Biggest Struggle:

_____

_____

_____

_____

_____

Where I Saw God Working:

_____

_____

_____

_____

_____

Bible Verse that Moved Me:

_____

_____

_____

_____

_____

What I'm Carrying into Next Week:

_____

_____

_____

_____

_____

10 Ways to Surrender Throughout the Week

☐ 1. Start the day with prayer instead of phone scrolling

☐ 2. Hand over one worry in prayer

☐ 3. Take a break when overwhelmed and invite God into the chaos

☐ 4. Speak kindly when it's hard

☐ 5. Let go of needing to be right

☐ 6. Say 'no' when it's the healthier choice

☐ 7. Trust God's timing — not your own

☐ 8. Ask for help

☐ 9. Extend grace to yourself

☐ 10. Praise God in the middle of a mess

Gratitude List

1._____

_____

2._____

_____

3._____

_____

4._____

_____

5._____

_____

Weekly Memory Verse Challenge

Write this week's memory verse below. Decorate it. Doodle it. Memorize it. Make it yours!

Memory Verse:

_____

_____

_____

_____

_____

_____

Doodle space:

Week 2

Drop the Baggage - Surrender and Trust

Let's be real: most of us are control freaks in cute church cardigans. But this week? We're done dragging our overloaded emotional carry-ons through life. God doesn't need our micromanaging. Lay it down. Let it go. Rip the duct tape off that box you stuffed your issues into and hand it to Jesus. He's already got a plan — and spoiler alert — it's way better than yours.

Guided Prayer to Start the Week

Lord, You already know how tightly I cling to things I was never meant to carry. Help me surrender my worries, my plans, my pride — and trust that You are better at being God than I am. Amen.

Day 1 — 10 Things I Can't Live Without

1. & 2. <u>WD-40 and Duct Tape</u>: You've all heard the saying: If it doesn't move but should, use WD-40; if it moves but shouldn't, use duct tape." Love it.

3. <u>Music</u>: I truly don't understand when people say, "I don't like (or listen to) music" There is music out there for every mood I'm in and for every experience I have had... music is one of the most important things in my life. I was born in 1970, so, I can go from 50s doo-wop to 70s yacht and classic rocks, but I can't live without my 80s new wave and 90s hiphop/dance jams... did I mention I love rap?

4. <u>My cell phone</u>: I'm a gadget geek; I admit it! Some people will think this is very sad, but I thrive on instant communication and endless entertainment. I think technology is amazing and, since it's constantly evolving and advancing, perhaps it's also representative of how we should be, too. I guess what I'm saying is that, if I can get excited about new technology and exploring its possibilities and capabilities, I should be able to accept similar changes in my life and willingly (and gladly) move forward in life. God WANTS us to embrace change. It's all about HIS WILL and He tells us in His Word:

> *"Do not be conformed to this world, but be transformed by the renewal of your mind, that by testing you may discern what is the will of God, what is good and acceptable and perfect."* Romans 12:2

"Remember not the former things; nor consider the things of old. Behold, I am doing a new thing! Now it springs forth; do you not perceive it? I will make a way in the wilderness and rivers in the desert." Isaiah 43:18-19

5 & 6. <u>Velcro and Bungee Cords</u>: self-explanatory

7. <u>Furry family members</u>: Chester, Pippa, Pax, Jazz, Buddy, and my grand-doggos, Bailey and Moose...the first 3 have already gone to Heaven... Moose is the baby of the family now.

8. <u>Amazon</u>: I truly cannot survive without it... be honest, could YOU live without it? Amazon is like my personal genie, ready to grant my shopping wishes in the blink of an eye. With just a few clicks, I can explore a world of endless options, often at prices that won't break the bank, and they will miraculously appear on my doorstep, many times on the same day or first thing in the morning!

This past Lenten season I gave up Amazon. I did well, but let me just say this: I'm a sinner

9. <u>My Brother P-Touch labeler</u>: if you do not yet have one, go out NOW and get one (or get one on Amazon – see #8)! I'll wait. Go ahead!

Just a couple of examples of how utterly important it is to have one: 1. labeling the cords that go into the surge suppressor where your computer is plugged AND all those pesky cords behind the TV and 2. labeling containers of MY food so no one else dips into it (Who am I kidding? They do anyway LOL.) Brother P-Touch Label Maker: about $30

10. <u>Chocolate</u>: especially the kind you get at a real chocolate shop (like the Sayville Chocolatier, Kilwin's in Patchogue or Roger's Frigate in Port Jefferson) where you can pick one of everything and have it wrapped up pretty in a box. Then, the problem: you don't know which to eat first, the cashew turtles, the huge M&M topped peanut buttercup, the homemade, dark chocolate-covered graham cracker, the peppermint patty, the coconut cluster or... really, do I have to explain more? Ugh, I have to stop.

I'm sure there are plenty of things I could write about here, but I just wanted to write something and get the creative juices to start flowing with this whole theme of God's gifts. What's crazy is that, as I'm writing all of this, I, myself, am learning about what God intends for me and how I live my life. He gave us all these amazing things that I listed above, plus a whole lot more! I could probably write an entire book only on the topic of things I like and whether or not it pleases God.

I urge you to make your own list of favorite things (aka blessings). Doesn't matter the order in which they appear, just that you give them some thought. Write them in your notebook and do a quick web search for "Bible verses about". Jot some down and pray on them, asking for His guidance in how HE wants you to feel. My guess is that He probably thinks duct tape, WD-40, Velcro, and bungee cords are cool.

> *"For where your treasure is, there your heart will be also."* Matthew 6:21

Today I'm Feeling:

_____

Today's Struggle:

_____

Small Victory Today:

_____

Where I Saw God Today:

_____

Prayer for Today:

_____

_____

_____

_____

_____

Reflect: What items, habits, or comforts might I be relying
on more than God?

_____

_____

_____

_____

_____

Chapter Reflection: How does what I cling to reveal what I trust?

_____

_____

_____

_____

_____

Journal

_____

_____

_____

_____

_____

_____

_____

Doodle space:

Day 2 — So Blessed I Could Burst

I got applause again yesterday. That's twice now—for my presentation on cyberbullying and internet safety. And let me tell you, after decades of teaching, not once had I ever been applauded after a class. But here I am—getting claps, laughs, lingering questions, and even a few wide eyes.

And honestly? It feels amazing. I felt good at what I do. What a blessing!

Let's be real—most people would rather sit through a root canal than attend a workplace workshop. They're usually watching the clock, wondering if they can sneak out early or they're just mentally checking out. Not mine. My workshop is a jam-packed two-hour session—twice the length of most— and no one's begging to leave early. If anything, they stay late to talk, to connect, to share. And every time that happens, I know this isn't just my job—it's my calling. God placed this message in my heart for such a time as this. (Esther 4:14, anyone?)

Yesterday, one of those post-class lingerers asked me to join his new company. He's building something big, and he wants me to help lead the charge against bullying. He said I was passionate, well-spoken, and exactly the kind of voice he needed. Today he followed up—wants to meet and get started. That's not just a pat on the back. That's purpose.

That's God opening a new door.

Later that same day, I was called to translate a phone call to a parent.

Nothing fancy—just some questions about a student's behavior at home. At one point, when the counselor asked if the boy helped with chores, the dad let out this big, joyful belly laugh. We all laughed right along with him. It was a simple moment, but rich with humanity. Later, the counselor emailed every one of my supervisors, thanking me for stepping in last-minute and doing such a great job. I felt seen. Useful. Blessed to be a blessing.

Fifth period rolled around, and my friend popped into my classroom out of the blue. She never does that. Turns out, she'd meant to give me a birthday gift back in November but hadn't gotten the chance. Yet here she was—right when my heart needed a little lift—handing me the cutest cowboy boot keychain. I clipped it to my keys immediately. That tiny gift felt like God whispering, I see you. I haven't forgotten.

Later that night, I had the most honest, loving conversation with my dad—the kind we hadn't had in ages. There was connection, depth, grace. I went to bed with a full heart, thankful for reconciliation and peace. That, too, is the hand of God at work. And this morning? My sweet, little one brought over one of those old-school, folded-paper fortune-tellers I made for her. You know the kind—open, close, open, close— and a message appears inside. Mine read: "You are very loved."

She looked up at me with the most sincere little smile and said, "You ARE!" Instant tears. So many blessings in one tiny moment coming from my tiny human!

Today, I am overflowing. I know who I am—not because of applause, promotions, or keychains, or what a folded-paper toy tells me—but because God continues to pour out kindness upon kindness.

I am appreciated.

Honored.

Needed.

I felt "smart", "articulate", and "funny" ... And above all else, I feel *loved beyond belief*—not just by people, but by the God who made me, walks with me, and delights in me.

> *"For from His fullness we have all received, grace upon grace."* John 1:16

And grace upon grace it is.

> *"Every good and perfect gift is from above..."* James 1:17

Today I'm Feeling:

_____

Today's Struggle:

_____

Small Victory Today:

_____

Where I Saw God Today:

_____

Prayer for Today:

_____

_____

_____

_____

_____

Reflect: What are three specific blessings I've taken for granted lately?

_____

_____

_____

_____

_____

Chapter Reflection: How does recognizing my blessings shape my attitude toward surrender?

_____

_____

_____

_____

_____

Journal

_____

_____

_____

_____

_____

_____

_____

_____

_____

Doodle space:

Day 3 — A Fresh Coat of Paint

Scenario: you decide to paint your bedroom.

You remove everything but the bed, spackle the walls three times, cut in all the corners, apply the new color, and paint the trim white to erase that horrible color that was there before. Everything gets put away — brushes, rollers, paint trays, ladder — and you step back...

Wow

How did I not do this sooner? Hold up, there's gotta be a Bible verse for this.

> *"Therefore, if anyone is in Christ, he is a new creation: The old has passed away; behold, the new has come"*
> 2 Corinthians 5:17

You start moving things back into the room: nightstands, hamper, one dresser, then the second... but what's this? Wow, I can't believe I still have that old shirt; it doesn't even fit me anymore because it shrunk so badly.

Why was I keeping it?

Wait — another decrepit shirt!

Why was I keeping THAT? I wonder if there's a Bible verse...

> *"...to put off your old self, which belongs to your former manner of life and is corrupt through deceitful desires, and to be renewed in the spirit of your minds,"*
> Ephesians 4:22–23

Before you know it, you're grabbing contractor bags and loading them with donations and garbage. It becomes addicting, this cleansing and purging. So, you move on to the kids' rooms.

This doesn't fit, that will never be worn, they never play with this anymore, there are too many pieces missing from that game. Why does my daughter try to recycle every toilet paper tube and twist tie that enters this house?

Is that a candy wrapper from Halloween (six months ago)??

Ugh... can I get a Bible verse here?

> *"Therefore, since we are surrounded by so great a cloud of witnesses, let us also lay aside every weight, and sin which clings so closely, and let us run with endurance the race that is set before us"* Hebrews 12:1

Three days and several contractor bags later, you step back again and feel lighter with an overwhelming sense of satisfaction in your newly organized home. Nothing quite compares to it.

This was how I spent the last week or so. I can actually say that I accomplished something big this vacation week.

However, the desire to clean and purge is still with me. I reiterate:

> *"Remember not the former things, nor consider the things of old. Behold, I am doing a new thing; now it springs forth, do you not perceive it? I will make a way in the wilderness and rivers in the desert"* Isaiah 43:18–19

What could be next? My guess is there's a lesson here in letting go of my old, sinful ways and putting on the "cloak of righteousness."

> *"See, I am doing a new thing! Now it springs up; do you not perceive it?"* Isaiah 43:19

Today I'm Feeling:

_____

Today's Struggle:

_____

Small Victory Today:

_____

Where I Saw God Today:

_____

Prayer for Today:

_____

_____

_____

_____

_____

Reflect: Where is God calling me to renew or let go of something old?

_____

_____

_____

_____

_____

Chapter Reflection: What am I still trying to cover up that God wants to fully transform?

_____

_____

_____

_____

_____

Journal

_____

_____

_____

_____

_____

_____

_____

_____

_____

_____

Doodle space:

Day 4 — Strengthened by Our Weakness (and Our Chocolate Cravings)

This past Sunday's sermon title hit me right between the eyes: Strengthened by Our Weakness.

In church, we heard the familiar story: Adam and Eve, staring at that one stupid tree out of all the thousands God gave them, and — surprise! — they couldn't resist. Meanwhile, in the Gospel lesson, Jesus walks into the wilderness, gets tempted three times by Satan himself, and just hands Satan his hat. I mean, He doesn't just resist — He rebukes, quotes Scripture, and basically tells him to take a hike. Wouldn't it be nice if it were that easy for the rest of us?

Temptation?

Yeah, it's probably the well-established root system of half my problems... and a good chunk of the other half, too. Let's start small: Chocolate.

Listen, I have a long, tragic history with chocolate. It's basically my personal forbidden fruit. In my wilder days (read: last Tuesday), I was known to keep a stash in my desk like a squirrel prepping for winter. Now? I resist. I try to be responsible. I redirect myself to wholesome activities like laundry or doing the dishes... (Okay, let's be real: I *think* about doing laundry and dishes. Mostly I whine internally and pray for strength. *pops 2 Milk Duds in mouth*)

However, temptation isn't just about sweets. It's everywhere. It's in my pride, my impatience, my need for approval.

Honestly? Chocolate is easy to walk past some days. My pride? Not so much. Let me tell you about the Great Grad School Obsession.

I went back to school as a working adult, married and pregnant with my first child. This wasn't "undergrad-me" who cared more about weekends than GPAs.

No, this time it was I had to get A's. Not wanted — HAD TO.

I even filed a complaint over one A- (and yes, I still think I was right...mostly... sort of... maybe).

Lord, have mercy.

Fast forward to now: I give workshops for colleagues, and guess what? Evaluations! Seven categories! In eleven workshops, every attendee rated me "Excellent" across the board — except ONE PERSON who, for EVERY workshop I give, dared give me... "Good." Not even "Very Good." Just "Good." Say what now?

And what did I do? Did I smile and humbly thank God for the opportunity to serve? Nope. I fumed about it as though I had dropped my lollipop in the dirt.

> *"Pride goes before destruction, and a haughty spirit before a fall."* Proverbs 16:18

Ouch.

Turns out, perfectionism isn't just a cute personality quirk — it's a big old temptation wrapped in a socially acceptable bow. My pride wants to be noticed, praised, validated. And if I'm being a faithful Lutheran about it: It's sin.

Full stop. No sugar-coating it. I don't need therapy for it (well...maybe a little). I need repentance.

And grace.

> *But he said to me, "My grace is sufficient for you, for my power is made perfect in weakness." Therefore, I will boast all the more gladly of my weaknesses, so that the power of Christ may rest upon me.* 2 Corinthians 12:9

Every Lent, I get reminded:

- I am dust
- I need Jesus
- I am not saved because I resist chocolate (or pride, or gossip, or self-pity) I am saved because He never once failed in the desert, or on the cross, or in the tomb
- I don't need to be the best
- I just need to be faithful

So, not just during Lent, but all year long, when temptation comes knocking — whether it's chocolate, Amazon, applause or that sweet little voice saying, "You deserve it..." I'm praying to answer back the way Jesus did:

"Be gone, Satan!" Matthew 4:10

And if I fall (because I will fall) I'll get backup, crawl back to the foot of the cross, and hear Him say again:

"It is finished."

Strengthened by my weakness? Yes, Lord. Because when I am weak, then I am strong — in You.

Today I'm Feeling:

_____

Today's Struggle:

_____

Small Victory Today:

_____

Where I Saw God Today:

_____

Prayer for Today:

_____

_____

_____

_____

_____

Reflect: What weakness am I still ashamed of that God wants to use?

_____

_____

_____

_____

_____

Chapter Reflection: How has God shown strength in my moments of surrender?

_____

_____

_____

_____

_____

Journal

_____

_____

_____

_____

_____

_____

_____

_____

_____

_____

_____

_____

_____

Doodle space:

Day 5 — Ain't No Mountain...

For he will command his angels concerning you to guard you in all your ways. Psalm 91:11

I read a devotion recently about facing a mountain (of worries, bills, relationships, etc.) that you have to climb. Think about how insanely difficult it is to climb a mountain, then think about how much easier it is to go forward just 5 feet. You KNOW you have to climb that mountain eventually, but wouldn't it be SO much more doable if you simply focused on the 5 feet in front of you?

You actually don't know what the path entails. It may be smooth; it may be rough terrain. You may find a gassed-up 4-wheeler that makes your journey entirely different than you thought it would be! (THAT would be cool!)

It's like that with our faith and how it helps us journey through life with all its ups and downs. God knows your mountain. He knows EVERY. SINGLE. STEP. you are going to take as you face that mountain. He is WITH YOU as you take those steps. He may even have a plan to change your route!

Do you know what tomorrow's route has in store? Nope. So, why worry about it today? Focus on the 5 feet ahead (you know, the ones you agreed at the beginning are doable?)! Know in your heart that God's got this. He will guide you and protect you! You just need to trust that He knows where you're headed when you don't.

Therefore, do not be anxious about tomorrow, for tomorrow will be anxious for itself. Sufficient for the day is its own trouble. Matthew 6:34

Be blessed today and don't be afraid to take a few steps toward your mountain.

Peace.

Today I'm Feeling:

_____

Today's Struggle:

_____

Small Victory Today:

_____

Where I Saw God Today:

_____

Prayer for Today:

_____

_____

_____

_____

Reflect: What "mountain" in my life do I need to stop climbing and start trusting God to move?

_____

_____

_____

_____

_____

Chapter Reflection: What would change if I fully believed God is bigger than my biggest obstacle?

_____

_____

_____

_____

_____

Journal

_____

_____

_____

_____

_____

_____

_____

_____

_____

_____

Doodle space:

Day 6 — Being Good (Or Trying Really, Really Hard)

Do not be conformed to this world, but be transformed by the renewal of your mind, that by testing you may discern what is the will of God, what is good and acceptable and perfect. Romans 12:2

Let's be honest. You know that moment—you're in the turn lane, waiting patiently (like the good, law-abiding citizen you are), and someone comes flying up the right side, cuts you off, nearly takes off your bumper, and sails through the intersection like they own the road. You slam the brakes, lay on the horn, and before your brain can intervene... a few choice words exit your mouth like they've been waiting for this moment.

Been there? Yeah, me too. Often.

Now take a second and read Romans 12:2 again. Feeling good about how you handled that situation? Probably not. I certainly wasn't. Not proud of how I've handled plenty of moments like that. My mouth gets ahead of my soul, and unfortunately, it's usually faster than prayer.

Still, there's hope.

This verse reminds us that we don't have to stay stuck in those reactions. God wants to transform us—not just slap a filter on our mouths, but to truly renew our minds. He invites us into a new way of thinking, one shaped by His truth, not by this impatient, angry world.

I need this daily. Scratch that—I need this hourly. In the heat of frustrating, unfair, or just plain rude moments, I'm learning to stop and put my focus on God. I pray. I plead. Sometimes I whine. My mind needs a total refresh, and only the Holy Spirit can do that kind of rewiring.

Yes, I'm human. Yes, I mess up. Often. Yet I'm not without hope, because I am a forgiven sinner, daily drenched in grace. Even when I fall short (again), God doesn't roll His eyes and walk away. He stays. He works. He changes me little by little.

Here's the truth: I struggle with being "good." Like, *really* struggle. I sin like a pro. What I can't do on my own is live up to God's standard of goodness. That's where the surrender comes in. My thoughts don't naturally lean toward the "holy". They lean toward snark, sarcasm, and self-defense. That's why I need His thoughts to become my thoughts. Because only good things can come from God-pleasing, Spirit-led thinking.

When my mind is focused on Him, everything else, even my reactions, starts to follow. I need a prayer... you?

Father God,

You know me inside and out—my flaws, my tendencies, my triggers— and You still love me. Thank You for Your patience and mercy that never run out, even when my temper does. I ask You to transform my thoughts. Rewire my reactions. Help me think the way You think, and to respond with grace, even when my flesh wants to honk the horn and yell. Remind me daily that I am a forgiven sinner, not because I'm good, but because You are. Continue to shape me, Lord. Help me to seek what is good, what is pleasing to You, and what is perfect. Make my thoughts a place where Your Spirit is welcome.

In Jesus' name I pray, Amen.

"If righteousness could be gained through the law, Christ died for nothing!" Galatians 2:21

Today I'm Feeling:

_____

Today's Struggle:

_____

Small Victory Today:

_____

Where I Saw God Today:

_____

Prayer for Today:

_____

_____

_____

_____

_____

Reflect: Where am I striving for approval instead of resting in grace?

_____

_____

_____

_____

_____

Chapter Reflection: How does surrendering the need to be perfect free me to walk with God honestly?

_____

_____

_____

_____

Journal

_____

_____

_____

_____

_____

_____

_____

_____

_____

Doodle space:

Day 7 — Detours, Distractions, and Divine Grace

Commit your work to the Lord, and your plans will be established. Proverbs 16:3

Funny thing happened to me on the way to the kitchen...

We had just returned from a spontaneous little getaway—one night at the Marriott with our girls and some family friends. It was fun, restful, and exactly what we needed. But the moment I stepped back into the house around 11:30 a.m., real life hit me like a pile of unfolded laundry.

I had a list longer than my arm: bake a lemon meringue pie (thank you, Aunt Peg, for the recipe!) for a dinner party, pay the parks fee so we could book our camping trip, vacuum, clean the bathroom, fold laundry, make beds, file paperwork...and those are just the ones I remember.

Well, the pie got made. So did some chocolate-covered strawberries. I even managed to update the antivirus software on my computer while the lemon was simmering and empty the dishwasher while the meringue was baking. Somewhere in there, I prepped lunches for the girls, too.

Victory!

Ok, I lied, here's what really happened: I'd start one task—say, sorting papers on the dining room table—and halfway through, I'd remember I needed a trash bag.

...which meant walking through the house

...which meant getting distracted by five other messes or chores screaming my name.

Before I knew it, I had barely half-finished tasks in every room, the house looked worse than before, and I was no longer sure that I had even started. Sound familiar?

Life can feel a lot like that sometimes... scattered, overwhelming, pulled in a dozen directions with nothing quite finished (amirite, ladies?).

But the Lord isn't surprised by our chaos. He meets us in it. Multitasking and procrastination might be part of my wiring, but God's grace weaves through it all. Even in the distractions, He is working on me and through me. Even in the detours, He is guiding me and blessing me. Even when our to-do lists are unfinished, His plan is right on schedule.

Sometimes I think God uses these messy, chaotic moments to remind us: you're not the one holding it all together—I am. And thank goodness for that.

So today, instead of beating myself up for the mess, I'm choosing to give thanks for what was accomplished, and trust that tomorrow will hold enough grace for what's left.

Lord, thank You for being present in the mess of my every day. In my half-done tasks and my distracted mind, help me to remember that Your plans for me are never derailed. Teach me to commit even the smallest chores to You and trust that You're working through it all.

Amen

> *"In their hearts humans plan their course, but the Lord establishes their steps."* Proverbs 16:9

Today I'm Feeling:

_____

Today's Struggle:

_____

Small Victory Today:

_____

Where I Saw God Today:

_____

Prayer for Today:

_____

_____

_____

_____

_____

Reflect: What detour in my life has actually led to grace?

_____

_____

_____

_____

Chapter Reflection: How has God used an unexpected path to draw me closer to Him?

_____

_____

_____

_____

_____

Journal

_____

_____

_____

_____

_____

_____

_____

_____

Doodle space:

Weekly Reflection

What did I finally let go of this week?

_____

_____

_____

_____

_____

How did God show me He's in control?

_____

_____

_____

_____

_____

_____

Where did I feel peace after surrendering?

_____

_____

_____

End-of-Week Reflection

Biggest Growth Moment:

_____

_____

_____

_____

_____

Biggest Struggle:

_____

_____

_____

_____

_____

Where I Saw God Working:

_____

_____

_____

_____

Bible Verse that Moved Me:

_____

_____

_____

_____

_____

What I'm Carrying into Next Week:

_____

_____

_____

_____

_____

10 Ways to Surrender Throughout the Week

☐ 1. Start the day with prayer instead of phone scrolling

☐ 2. Hand over one worry in prayer

☐ 3. Take a break when overwhelmed and invite God into the chaos

☐ 4. Speak kindly when it's hard

☐ 5. Let go of needing to be right

☐ 6. Say 'no' when it's the healthier choice

☐ 7. Trust God's timing — not your own

☐ 8. Ask for help

☐ 9. Extend grace to yourself

☐ 10. Praise God in the middle of a mess

Gratitude List

1._____

_____

2._____

_____

3._____

_____

4._____

_____

5._____

_____

Weekly Memory Verse Challenge

Write this week's memory verse below. Decorate it. Doodle it. Memorize it. Make it yours!

Memory Verse:

_____

_____

_____

_____

Doodle space:

Week 3

Patchwork & Grace--Healing and Restoration

Cue the ugly cries and the holy Band-Aids. This week we admit that we're a little (okay, a lot) broken — and invite God to do His sacred stitching.

No, He's not angry with you. He's not surprised by your mess. And yes, He still calls you His. Let His grace meet you in the soft spots where you've been aching too long.

Guided Prayer to Start the Week

God of mercy, I hand You the places that still ache — the wounds I hide, the fears I carry, and the stories that still sting. Stitch grace into every tear and make something beautiful out of what's been broken. Amen.

"Come to me, all who labor and are heavy laden, and I will give you rest. Take my yoke upon you, and learn from me, for I am gentle and lowly in heart, and you will find rest for your souls. For my yoke is easy, and my burden is light." Matthew 11:28-30

Let's do this.

Day 1 — Phobias and Panic Attacks

"For I am the Lord your God who takes hold of your right hand and says to you, Do not fear; I will help you." Isaiah 41:13

That's Petey. A cute little clipart of the real Petey. I find it easier to look at this picture as opposed to the other picture I downloaded of a real mouse. Today, during first period, out of the corner of my eye I saw a little field mouse scurry across the edge of the room. I instantly went into panic mode and had a full-blown anxiety attack. My heart began to beat faster, I got extremely lightheaded, I was almost hyperventilating.

What was most shocking about my reaction was that it was completely involuntary. I never expected it to happen, and I couldn't stop it. So, my friend and colleague helped me out and stayed in the room until the end of the class. I had to get out of there. I walked around the school a bit and had the nurse check my blood pressure (for which I was on medicine at the time) and it was 164 / 96. Not great. I did some deep breathing.

Anyway, the class named the mouse "Petey."

Why in the world did I freak out like I did? The only thing I can think of is that it all stems from when I was a kid. At about age 13, I was home alone while my parents were out. I was in the den watching a movie and out of the corner of my eye (much like how it happened today) I saw a small mouse run along the baseboard of the room. I was alone and got pretty freaked out, not knowing what to do. Also, during those years of mice in the house, I would lie in bed listening to the scritch-scritch-scritch and scurrying of mice inside the walls of my bedroom.

Again, freaked out, I couldn't do anything about it. However, Dad set up traps in the attic with peanut butter and, on more than one occasion, I encountered a trapped one. The images have stayed with me all of these years, etched on my brain.

I love nature, I love animals. I even like looking at the little mice in the pet store. The difference is they are in a glass tank. I don't like bugs, but they are more afraid of people than we are of them, so they don't bother me as much. However, aren't mice supposed to be hidden from "the public?" They are not supposed to be in my classroom, that's for sure.

Why DO we have fears and phobias?

Most of the phobias that I saw on www.phobialist.com were ridiculous:

- fear of bellybuttons: omphalophobia
- fear of the figure 8: octophobia
- fear of long words: hippopotomonstrosesquipedaliophobia (ironic)
- fear of mice: musophobia, muriphobia, or suriphobia (why three names?)

I'm now accepting the fact that I'm a normal person with a phobia. One in ten people have a phobia, you know. I learned that today after a little research. Perhaps it will prove to be temporary, as in the past I have had a fear of crossing bridges (gephyrophobia) and going through tunnels (why is there no name for that?), but not much anymore. What could possibly be next? Please, not xocolatophobia (fear of chocolate!)

Biblical Verses on Fear for us to Ponder

> *"fear not, for I am with you; be not dismayed, for I am your God I will strengthen you, I I will help you, I will uphold you with my righteous right hand"* Isaiah 41:10

> *"...do not be anxious about anything, but in everything by prayer and supplication with thanksgiving let your requests be made known to God. And the peace of God, which surpasses all understanding, will guard your hearts and your minds in Christ Jesus."* Philippians 4:6-7

> *"I sought the Lord, and he answered me and delivered me from all my fears."* Psalm 34:4

Christian Ways to Cope with Fear

(according to the stuff I found on the interwebs)

- Prayer: Take time to pray about your fears. Share your anxieties with God and ask for His strength.
- Scripture Meditation: Reflect on the verses above. Write them down and keep them where you can see them.
- Community Support: Talk to friends, family, or a church group about your fears. Sharing can lighten your burden.
- Mindfulness and Breathing: Practice deep breathing techniques, possibly incorporating prayer or scripture during these moments.
- Journaling: Write about your fears and how they make you feel. Documenting can help to process emotions.

Incorporating these tips can help turn fear into faith, allowing for a more peaceful mindset!

Today I'm Feeling:

_____

Today's Struggle:

_____

Small Victory Today:

_____

Where I Saw God Today:

_____

Prayer for Today:

_____

_____

_____

_____

_____

Reflect: What fear has been gripping me lately?

_____

_____

_____

_____

_____

Chapter Reflection: How is God calling me to breathe, trust, and receive His peace?

_____

_____

_____

_____

_____

Journal

_____

_____

_____

_____

_____

_____

_____

_____

_____

Doodle space:

Day 2 — Insomnia

Here I lie, 3:29 a.m., wide awake, writing because I need something to do.

I haven't written in a while — took a little mental health sabbatical to get some junk sorted out upstairs (my brain). (Highly recommend.)

I don't know why, but lately I've been waking up around 3 a.m. most mornings. Stress? Anxiety? The laundry pile mocking me from across the hall? Probably yes to all of the above.

> *"casting all your anxieties on Him, because He cares for you."* 1 Peter 5:7

So OK, fine, I have a few things on my mind:

- My daughter and her O.D.D. behavior that's got me praying for the fruit of the Spirit every five minutes
- The dog's checkup (where is that license renewal?)
- Bills (ugh)
- Two playdates (can kids just entertain themselves for once?)
- Dye Easter eggs (because apparently, it's a national crisis if we don't)
- And for the love of Pete, fold the laundry, woman!!!

But the Lord answered her, "Martha, Martha, you are anxious and troubled about many things, but one thing is necessary." Luke 10:41–42

Yeah... My life sounds pretty typical, right?

I feel like all I do is trudge through each day, dragging myself from task to task like a tired pack mule. No real incentive, no confetti raining from the sky when I cross anything off my list. What's the prize? Why do I need a prize?

Well, that's just me and my selfishness talking... (And yes, I checked— trudge is a word. Merriam-Webster says so.)

> *"Do all things without grumbling or disputing, that you may be blameless and innocent, children of God without blemish in the midst of a crooked and twisted generation, among whom you shine as lights in the world."* Philippians 2:14–15

Cue the Holy Spirit smacking me upside the head because, hey, guess what week it is (well, when I wrote this)? It's Holy Week — the most important, heavy, beautiful, heart-wrecking, soul-lifting week of the year.

It's the week that reminds me that my trudging is NOTHING compared to what Jesus carried to that cross: that beyond heavy, wooden cross, His own blood-soaked, striped skin, and the most painful of all, my sin.

Twelve years ago, I made a very personal, spiritual walk through Holy Week. Every day, I read the Gospel accounts of Jesus's journey— step by bloody step — to His death and resurrection. That Saturday (Easter Vigil), I drove out to the Shinnecock Canal, found a little beach nearby, threw down a blanket, cracked open my Bible, and finished the story:

He rose! He lives!

And not just lives — He conquered death FOR ME! For this tired, stressed-out, laundry-buried, coffee-fueled woman lying awake at 3:49 a.m.

> *Jesus said to her, "I am the resurrection and the life. Whoever believes in me, though he die, yet shall he live, "* John 11:25

That journey through repentance, reflection, and gritty reality led me to the real prize: *Undeserved, eternal life with my Savior and God.*

> *"I have fought the good fight, I have finished the race, I have kept the faith. Henceforth there is laid up for me the crown of righteousness..."* 2 Timothy 4:7– 8

So here I lie, 3:55 a.m., and you know what? I can finally go to sleep now.

I realize just how blessed I am.

I will continue this walk with Christ — not trudging, not dragging, but running with joy in my heart.

He is my Prize.

> *"In peace I will lie down and sleep, for you alone, Lord, make me dwell in safety."* Psalm 4:8

Today I'm Feeling:

_____

Today's Struggle:

_____

Small Victory Today:

_____

Where I Saw God Today:

_____

Prayer for Today:

_____

_____

_____

_____

_____

Reflect: What thoughts keep me up at night?

_____

_____

_____

_____

_____

Chapter Reflection: How can I invite God into even the sleepless hours?

_____

_____

_____

_____

Journal

_____

_____

_____

_____

_____

_____

_____

_____

_____

Doodle space:

Day 3 — PAT

Rejoice always, pray without ceasing, give thanks in all circumstances; for this is the will of God in Christ Jesus for you. 1 Thessalonians 5:16-18

Years ago, I went to a workshop with the church. One of the things we learned was "how to" pray. Sure, it sounds weird to say someone needs to be "taught" how to pray, sometimes the best prayers are simply when you talk freely to God, telling Him how you feel or what you need.

In the same way, the Spirit helps us in our weakness. We do not know what we ought to pray for, but the Spirit himself intercedes for us (see Romans 8:26). However, from that workshop I attended, I learned a great "trick" to saying a quick and easy prayer: PAT.

Praise: tell God how awesome He is! Let Him know how you feel about Him!

Ask: ask God for forgiveness. Being omniscient, He knows what sins you hold (Oh, yes, He does! Yup - even THAT); even things of which you aren't aware! So, don't worry if you can't remember everything; He knows, trust me on this. HOWEVER! Our Father in Heaven is merciful and full of grace! Also, ask God for what you feel you need, but always remember that it is His will; ask Him to help you accept this!

Thank: thank God for all the blessings He has given you! That's the easy part!

The Lord has heard my plea; the Lord accepts my prayer. Psalm 6:9

I call upon you, for you will answer me, O God; incline your ear to me; hear my words. Psalm 17:6

And whatever you ask in prayer, you will receive, if you have faith. Matthew 21:22

When my girls went to Emanuel Lutheran School from preschool through elementary, I had the honor to attend their Wednesday morning chapel service. The students lead the prayers in their own signature style:

- We praise God, You are...
- We repent and are sorry for ...
- We pray for ...

Sound familiar? We can learn something from the children and how they pray: be honest, be simple, and speak from the heart. Remember PAT!

We praise You, oh God. You are awesome, amazing, the rock that never fails! We repent and are sorry for our sins. We thank you for always listening to and answering our prayers. We pray for those who are sick, our soldiers and all whom we love. Lord in Your mercy, hear our prayer.

"The Spirit himself intercedes for us through wordless groans." Romans 8:26

Today I'm Feeling:

_____

Today's Struggle:

_____

Small Victory Today:

_____

Where I Saw God Today:

_____

Prayer for Today:

_____

_____

_____

_____

Reflect: What's been too heavy for words lately?

_____

_____

_____

_____

Chapter Reflection: How does knowing the Spirit prays for me give me strength to keep going?

_____

_____

_____

_____

Journal

_____

_____

_____

_____

_____

_____

_____

_____

Doodle Space:

Day 4 — Friendship

This chapter is dedicated to my beautiful friend group: "Ladies Who Lunch", or as Eric affectionately calls it "Chicks Who Chow", "Dames Who Dine", and "Gals Who Graze".

Did your child do something awesome? Are you celebrating getting a new job? Did you pass a difficult test? Get the all-clear for beating cancer? What joy! Thanks be to God! Why not share this joy with those you love! Together you can celebrate by praising God for all of your blessings and good will!

When we are troubled, and troubled times DO come, we should also talk to those same friends. We know that, if we can unload our burdens, we'll feel better. True friends do not judge or criticize; they listen, understand and show empathy. They offer help. They are often the voice of reason when we're being unreasonable. Having friends in Christ gives an added bonus: prayer!

When I read this from a Christian pastor:

> *"Our greatest joys and our greatest sorrows will involve our friends. All of us have been places or done things which were absolutely wonderful, yet because we did not have a friend with us at the time to share it, the joy was not as great. We multiply our joy by being able to share it with friends either by having them with us to also experience it or by being able to tell them about it later."*

I understood it immediately regarding my Ladies group. It was perfectly stated!

However, who is our ultimate best friend? JESUS! He carries our burdens and also rejoices with us when we celebrate. Whether we are sad or happy, He is always there to listen to us. Lean on Him; He is our rock and as well as our salvation!

Having friends is yet another gift from God. Pray together, praise God together, celebrate together, cry together... Christian friends will ease your pain and add joy to your life!

Let's give Him some love... join me...

Dear Lord, we are so blessed to have friends with whom we can share our burdens and our joy. We thank you for not only our earthly friends, but Christ, our Best Friend. We ask that you continue to bless us with opportunities to multiply our joy and divide our grief. In Jesus' name we pray.

Amen

> *"Two are better than one... If either of them falls, one can help the other up."* Ecclesiastes 4:9-10

Today I'm Feeling:

_____

Today's Struggle:

_____

Small Victory Today:

_____

Where I Saw God Today:

_____

Prayer for Today:

_____

_____

_____

_____

_____

Reflect: Who has walked beside me in a season of
brokenness?

_____

_____

_____

_____

Chapter Reflection: How can I be that kind of friend to
someone else right now?

_____

_____

_____

Journal

_____

_____

_____

_____

_____

_____

_____

_____

_____

_____

Doodle space:

Day 5 — First Judas, Then Peter

So, along with my focus and meditation on Judas this Easter season (I got REALLY hung up and deeply pensive about Jesus washing Judas' feet even knowing of his imminent betrayal; HE WASHED HIS FEET!)

I now have this gem about Peter... You see, Peter was a dope... He said the wrong things, did the wrong things, and was just plain clueless...

SAME

In this lesson, Peter, blessed and filled with the Holy Spirit, lays it all out for the Sadducees, then he and John get released and walk out...

MIC DROP

There is hope and love and forgiveness ALL OVER THE PLACE in the Bible!

Let this bless you:

> *And when they had set them in the midst, they inquired, "By what power or by what name did you do this?" Then Peter, filled with the Holy Spirit, said to them, "Rulers of the people and elders, if we are being examined today concerning a good deed done to a crippled man, by what means this man has been healed, let it be known to all of you and to all the people of Israel that by the name of Jesus Christ of Nazareth, whom you crucified, whom God raised from the dead— by him this man is standing before*

you well. This Jesus is the stone that was rejected by you, the builders, which has become the cornerstone. And there is salvation in no one else, for there is no other name under heaven given among men by which we must be saved." Acts 4:7-12

In the end, Peter was the Rock. Ponder that.

"The Lord turned and looked straight at Peter... And he went outside and wept bitterly." Luke 22:61-62

Today I'm Feeling:

_____

Today's Struggle:

_____

Small Victory Today:

_____

Where I Saw God Today:

_____

Prayer for Today:

_____

_____

_____

_____

_____

Reflect: When have I felt the sting of failure or betrayal?

_____

_____

_____

_____

_____

Chapter Reflection: What would it look like to weep, release, and return to grace?

_____

_____

_____

_____

_____

Journal

_____

_____

_____

_____

_____

_____

_____

_____

_____

_____

Doodle space:

Day 6 — Hi, I'm Peter...

Hi, I'm Peter. I screw up and disappoint people. I have BIG trust issues, too.

I am Peter all over again... I woke up this morning thinking that every time I don't trust God, every time I don't show love, every time I let anger or rage control me, I nail Jesus to the cross... Over and over

I crucify Him again and again. Wasn't once enough? The pain, the suffering... He did it once FOR ALL, and yeah, for me (and YOU), too.

There are days when I feel I'm in a deep pit of despair and that I can't climb out. I WANT to. I TRY to. I know He wants me out of it. I know I can't do it alone. If I'd only reach up... He's reaching down to me.

However, our hands can't meet. I need help. I need a boost up. That's where faith and the Holy Spirit come in.

When Peter encountered Jesus on the water and was told to walk to Him ON THE WATER, he was like "Dude! You're nuts!" So, he gave it a shot and it worked... for a minute... then Peter realized what he was doing, probably yelled something like, "Holy cr@p!" then started to sink.

Jesus reached out to Peter and taught Peter a hard lesson in TRUST and FAITH.

Years ago, when I felt my faith had reached new heights, I was at the Pavilion Praise worship down at the beach in Ocean

Grove, NJ, and I heard the band play a song that would forever resonate through to my very core.

You call me out upon the waters

The great unknown where feet may fail

And there I find You in the mystery

In oceans deep

My faith will stand

The Hillsong United song "Oceans" has changed lives around the world. It's been calling me for years and I need to finally listen to it on a loop until I break from Satan's evil grip.

Something's got to change in a big way; I can't live like this anymore. I've got every reason to be praising God with a huge smile and blessed disposition.

I should be witnessing instead of withering. I should be loving instead of leaving. Part of the hope I have is that Peter got his act together in the end. I have a long way to go.

So, I will call upon Your name

And keep my eyes above the waves

When oceans rise, my soul will rest in Your embrace

For I am Yours and You are mine

Spirit lead me where my trust is without borders

Let me walk upon the waters

Wherever You would call me

Take me deeper than my feet could ever wander

And my faith will be made stronger

In the presence of my Savior

Every day is a new day to start anew. I was Peter yesterday and I'll be Peter again; I'm 100% sure of that. Not today, Satan. I'm reaching up to my Savior, my lifesaver who walks on water.

> *"And I tell you, you are Peter, and on this rock I will build my church, and the gates of hell shall not prevail against it."* Matthew 16:18

Today I'm Feeling:

_____

Today's Struggle:

_____

Small Victory Today:

_____

Where I Saw God Today:

_____

Prayer for Today:

_____

_____

_____

_____

_____

Reflect: When have I been forgiven and restored like Peter?

_____

_____

_____

_____

_____

Chapter Reflection: How is Jesus calling me to walk forward, not backward?

_____

_____

_____

_____

_____

Journal

_____

_____

_____

_____

_____

_____

_____

_____

_____

_____

Doodle space:

Day 7 — The One That Wandered

I was a lost sheep.

Not in a poetic, soft-focus Instagram caption kind of way.

Nope. Straight up wandered-off-the-cliff-while-the-other-sheep-were-being-obedient kind of lost.

I grew up going to a very conservative Lutheran church (still do... LCMS is my "crew"), every week, like clockwork. Baptized? Check. First Communion? Check. Confirmation? Yup. I had all the "good Christian girl" boxes ticked. On paper, I looked solid. But inside? Let's just say... I knew of God, but I didn't know Him. Not really. I didn't understand who He truly was— or what He had done for me.

Jesus put it like this:

> *"What do you think? If a man has a hundred sheep, and one of them has gone astray, does he not leave the ninety-nine on the mountains and go in search of the one that went astray? And if he finds it, truly, I say to you, he rejoices over it more than over the ninety-nine that never went astray."* Matthew 18:12–13

That was me. I was the one who wandered off—confused, self-reliant, full of pride, and thinking I had it all figured out. Spoiler alert: I didn't.

By age 27, life had flipped upside down and spit me out. I moved back in with my parents after living in Rhode Island since high school. I was starting over—physically, emotionally, and most definitely spiritually. I found myself back at my childhood church, only this time, I didn't just show up and sit in the pew. I was hungry for something deeper.

I dove in—headfirst.

Bible studies? Signed up.

Women' retreats? Yes, please.

Adult catechism? Bring it.

I even went to every single service (yes, even the early ones) trying to get it to sink in and stick.

Was I trying to figure God out? Oh yeah. Did I totally understand the Bible back then? Ha! Will I *ever*? t was like trying to read IKEA instructions in Hebrew. But I kept going.

Deep down, I knew I needed something more. I needed Him. I wasn't just looking for religion—I was desperate for relationship. For redemption. I needed my Shepherd who had come looking for me.

> *"'Rejoice with me, for I have found my sheep that was lost.' Just so, I tell you, there will be more joy in heaven over one sinner who repents than over ninety-nine righteous persons who need no repentance."* Luke 15:6–7

That verse? That's my story. If it's yours too, just know this: no matter how far you've wandered, no matter how "put together" your faith may have looked on the outside, Jesus came for you. And He's rejoicing— like, REALLY rejoicing— when you turn back toward Him.

Here's the best part? He never once gave up on me.

Not then. Not now. Not ever.

Take a little journey back to a cold Saturday morning, January 3, 1998, won't you? As I drove past my church and saw Pastor's car. I knew he used that time to practice his sermons in the sanctuary, but I saw him in his office, and I stopped. I needed to talk. I felt so lost. What happened next was the most unforgettable event of my life: my "epiphany", if you will, finally opening my eyes to God's amazing grace.

After we spoke for a bit, I paused, crinkled my forehead as I got deep in thought for a moment, and asked Pastor, "You mean, after all the horrible things I've said and done, just because I believe in Him and am truly sorry, HE FORGIVES ME?"

His quiet response, "NOW you've got it!"

I sobbed. Like ugly cry.

I finally understood that well-known verse:

> *"For God so loved the world, that he gave his only Son, that whoever believes in him should not perish but have eternal life."* John 3:16

I know I'm not worthy of His grace, yet He gives it to me freely, lovingly. I will praise Him forever because of the mercy He shows me on the daily. I was lost but have been found. I listen to my Father's voice and follow Him.

I gotta talk to Him...

Heavenly Father, Your grace is amazing! I know I am not worthy, yet you continue to forgive, love, and bless me. Help me to better understand your Word so I may continue to praise you and share your message of grace and mercy with others. In Jesus' name, Amen

Read this again:

> *"Doesn't he leave the ninety-nine in the open country and go after the lost sheep until he finds it?"* Luke 15:4

Today I'm Feeling:

_____

Today's Struggle:

_____

Small Victory Today:

_____

Where I Saw God Today:

_____

Prayer for Today:

_____

_____

_____

_____

_____

Reflect: Have I ever felt like the one that wandered?

_____

_____

_____

_____

_____

Chapter Reflection: How does it change things to know that Jesus comes looking for me?

_____

_____

_____

_____

_____

Weekly Reflection

Where did I notice God's healing hand this week?

_____

_____

_____

_____

What area still needs time, grace, or attention?

_____

_____

_____

_____

_____

Biggest Growth Moment:

_____

_____

_____

_____

_____

Biggest Struggle:

_____

_____

_____

_____

_____

Where I Saw God Working:

_____

_____

_____

_____

_____

Bible Verse that Moved Me:

_____

_____

_____

_____

_____

What I'm Carrying into Next Week:

_____

_____

_____

_____

_____

10 Ways to Surrender Throughout the Week

☐ 1. Start the day with prayer instead of phone scrolling

☐ 2. Hand over one worry in prayer

☐ 3. Take a break when overwhelmed and invite God into the chaos

☐ 4. Speak kindly when it's hard

☐ 5. Let go of needing to be right

☐ 6. Say 'no' when it's the healthier choice

☐ 7. Trust God's timing — not your own

☐ 8. Ask for help

☐ 9. Extend grace to yourself

☐ 10. Praise God in the middle of a mess

Gratitude List

1._____

_____

2._____

_____

3._____

_____

4._____

_____

5._____

_____

Weekly Memory Verse Challenge

Write this week's memory verse below. Decorate it. Doodle it. Memorize it. Make it yours!

Memory Verse:

_____

_____

_____

_____

_____

Doodle space:

Week 4

Faith in the Wild— Living it Out in Everyday Chaos

You've got kids screaming, a grocery cart with a bad wheel, a flat iron that gave up on you, and yet — here you are, trying to live like Jesus. This week is for the in-between moments, the "Why am I even doing this?" days. God is not just in the mountaintop worship — He's in your Target run, your traffic jam, and your burnt dinner. Let's find Him there.

Guided Prayer to Start the Week

Lord, meet me in the middle of my mess. Help me live out faith in the moments that feel the most unholy — the rushed, the loud, the ordinary.

Remind me that nothing is too small or too chaotic for You to be present in. Amen.

> *"Give thanks in all circumstances; for this is God's will for you in Christ Jesus."* 1 Thessalonians 5:18

Day 1 — God Moments

My dear friend and sister in Christ, Nancy, taught me this perfect little phrase: "God Moments." She and I worked together on a couple of Lenten devotional booklets for our church. Between the hours spent formatting, assigning dates, selecting Bible verses, and organizing prayers, we found ourselves constantly pausing to share stories—those sweet, subtle moments when we knew God was near. Those were our God Moments, and they shaped our walk as Christian women more than we realized.

I bet you have your own list of God Moments! You may not always notice them right away—but sometimes, when you reflect later, the light turns on and you know: "That was God."

> *"Surely the Lord is in this place, and I did not know it."*
> Genesis 28:16

Write them down! These are the little everyday miracles that God weaves into our lives—proof that He is near, that He sees us, and that He cares. Whether it's in a note-taking app on your phone or a $1 notebook from the Buck-and-a Quarter Store (fka the dollar store... thanks, inflation), jot down your moments. Better yet, search for Bible verses that match what you felt. Let Scripture bring clarity to your experience.

> *"Remember the wondrous works that He has done, His miracles, and the judgments He uttered"* 1 Chronicles 16:12

If you're crafty, grab a sketchbook and some pretty pens. Use colors and doodles and lettering to document your God

Moments. Keep one in the car, one by your nightstand, one tucked into your purse. God is everywhere... let yourself see Him in the details!

Take a little time to reflect on those moments that have shaped your heart—big or small. The moments that changed you, encouraged you, stopped you in your tracks, or left you weeping in your kitchen (been there). Pair them with verses. Pray over them. Reread them when you're feeling lost or overwhelmed. God speaks in stillness and surprise.

"Be still and know that I am God." Psalm 46:10

These moments are part of His plan. Every time you recognize them, you are stepping a little closer into His purpose for you. These are YOUR God Moments. They are personal, powerful, and precious.

Cherish them.

Here are just a few of mine:

- Hearing the perfect song lyric at the exact moment I needed to (often in the grocery store, am I really that old? My jams are now airing in the produce aisle?)
- Catching the glint of a stained-glass window on a quiet drive
- A Bible verse "coincidentally" popping up in my feed or reading
- Watching my little girl dance like no one's watching
- Hearing my oldest daughter sing with confidence and grace
- Seeing the leaves change and feeling that first crisp fall breeze (favorite season)

- Reading an inspirational quote at just the right time
- Realizing how God places people in my life—or gently removes them
- Hitting every green light (or every red one, for a reason... happened last week GRR)
- Feeling my dog's cold nose nudging my arm for a cuddle
- Counting the songs of the mockingbird who sings outside my window

Each one of these and countless others, a quiet whisper from heaven.

Let's Pray:

Heavenly Father,

Thank You for the gentle, beautiful reminders of Your presence. Open our eyes to the God Moments You so graciously place in our lives. Let us not overlook them or brush them off, rather receive them with gratitude and awe. Help us to record them, reflect on them, and draw near to You through them. Give us hearts that recognize Your hand in both the everyday and the extraordinary. May these moments be reminders of Your love, Your faithfulness, and Your constant care.

In Jesus' precious name, Amen.

> *"My presence will go with you, and I will give you rest."* Exodus 33:14

Today I'm Feeling:

_____

Today's Struggle:

_____

Small Victory Today:

_____

Where I Saw God Today:

_____

Prayer for Today:

_____

_____

_____

_____

Reflect: When did I last feel a holy nudge in my everyday life?

_____

_____

_____

_____

Chapter Reflection: What can I do to become more aware of the God moments I might be missing?

_____

_____

_____

_____

_____

Journal

_____

_____

_____

_____

_____

_____

_____

_____

_____

Doodle space:

Day 2 — God Bless You (No, really!)

"Bless you!"

"No, Mommy—you have to say, '*God* bless you!'"

Oh, to be corrected by a tiny theologian in glitter sneakers. My youngest daughter reminds me on the daily where my focus should be:

God's blessings, front and center.

The irony? I'm one of the people who introduced her to Jesus... but now she's the one keeping my own faith in check. (God's got jokes.) It reminds me of the passage in Mark:

> *And they were bringing children to him that he might touch them, and the disciples rebuked them. But when Jesus saw it, he was indignant and said to them, "Let the children come to me; do not hinder them, for to such belongs the kingdom of God. Truly, I say to you, whoever does not receive the kingdom of God like a child shall not enter it." And he took them in his arms and blessed them, laying his hands on them.* Mark 10:13–16

This is more than a sweet Sunday School story. As I believe and follow the practices of the Lutheran Church, this is a clear affirmation that children are included in God's Kingdom, not based on their works or intellect or ability to explain the doctrine of justification, but by grace alone. And let me tell you, these little ones can teach us big things.

From the moment I discovered my girls were on their way, I considered God's gifts to me. He knows them. He has always known them.

Unique. Precious. Completely covered by His grace.

> *"Before I formed you in the womb, I knew you..."*
> Jeremiah 1:5

That truth—that God knew them before I ever did—is both humbling and comforting. Especially when you're a new mom running on grace and 3 hours of sleep.

When my oldest was born, I was terrified to take her out in public before she was baptized. I knew she had been born into sin (Romans 5:12, anyone?), and I feared that if something unthinkable happened before she was baptized and brought into the family of God, then what? I knew of God's mercy, but I clung so tightly to the gifts He gives through the Sacraments—particularly the gift of Baptism, where God names us His own and washes us clean.

To comfort me and ease my mind (read: to shut me up) my pastor offered to baptize her in the hospital if it really was stressing me out, but I waited—though probably with more anxiety than necessary.

She was baptized on All Saints Sunday, and now that day holds double the meaning for me. A celebration of those who've gone before us and of the very moment my baby was marked as a Child of God.

Fast forward to baby #2. You know I couldn't just pick any day. I wanted her Baptism to be equally meaningful. So together with my pastor, we chose Easter Vigil—a night full of light, resurrection, and hope. Walking through Holy Week, then seeing my baby baptized as we moved from Christ's death to His rising? Tears. All of them. What better time to celebrate eternal life than at the very moment we remember Jesus conquered sin and death?

These moments—rooted in Word and Sacrament—are what we cling to in the faith. It's not about emotions or warm fuzzies (though I've had plenty). It's about God's action. His promises. His grace given freely to us—not earned, not deserved, just given.

Somehow, in the everyday chaos of motherhood and mismatched socks, my daughters still teach me. Whether it's through bold reminders to say, "God bless you," or quiet moments of trust, they remind me that faith doesn't have to be complicated. It just has to be real.

So today, whether you're wrangling kids, doubting your parenting, or just trying to remember what day it is—pause.

Remember that God's blessings aren't earned. They're already yours.

Now go ahead. Say it out loud:

God bless you. (Yes, really.)

Pray...

Father in Heaven, thank you for all the lessons in faith you provide for us, whether through a child or through worship.

Continue to bless us with these lessons and the ability to understand their value in our lives.

In Jesus' name, Amen

"The Lord bless you and keep you; the Lord make his face shine on you..." Numbers 6:24

Today I'm Feeling:

_____

Today's Struggle:

_____

Small Victory Today:

_____

Where I Saw God Today:

_____

Prayer for Today:

_____

_____

_____

_____

_____

Reflect: Who needs a blessing today — and can I be the one to speak it?

_____

_____

_____

_____

_____

_____

Chapter Reflection: How does acknowledging blessings shift my daily outlook?

_____

_____

_____

_____

_____

_____

Journal

_____

_____

_____

_____

_____

_____

_____

_____

_____

_____

_____

Doodle space:

Day 3 — Find a Penny, Preach a Prayer

You know how the saying goes: "Find a penny, pick it up... all day long you'll have good luck." Cute. But let's be real, there's no such thing as luck, and there's nothing like God's promises.

My friend, Laura, told me that every time she finds a penny, she looks at that little phrase stamped on it: "In God We Trust." And instead of thinking about luck or superstition, she lets that be her reminder to actually trust in the Lord—for guidance, for strength, for peace, for all the things.

Honestly? I love that. Isn't that what we all need? A pocket-sized reminder that God's got this? I've said this before; you know the verses:

> "Trust in the LORD with all your heart and do not lean on your own understanding; in all your ways acknowledge him, and he will make straight your paths." Proverbs 3:5–6

Easier said than done, I know. We like to think we trust God—until we're knee-deep in stress, elbow-deep in laundry, or stuck behind someone going 20 in a 45. (Sanctification takes time, okay?)

But God never changes. He's steady. He's faithful. And He always comes through... maybe not in the way we pictured, but always in the way that's best.

> "Those who know your name trust in you, for you, LORD, have not forsaken those who seek you." Psalm 9:10

So, the next time you spot a penny on the ground—don't roll your eyes and keep walking. Pick it up (yes, even if it's tails up... remember, we are NOT superstitious!). Hold it in your hand and let those four little words remind you of something way bigger than luck.

Say out loud (or whisper if you're in Target), "I trust in You, Lord." Then shoot up a quick prayer: thank Him, praise Him, or just ask for help making it through your to-do list without losing your Jesus Joy.

While pennies might not buy much these days (heck, they don't even mint them anymore, do they?), they can still remind us of something priceless.

Ooh... we need Him

Father in Heaven, I thank you for being there when I need You. I know I can always trust in Your will, that You will guide me and love me forever. Help me to share this message with those who need You. In Jesus' name, I pray.

Amen

> *"The heavens declare the glory of God; the skies proclaim the work of his hands."* Psalm 19:1

Today I'm Feeling:

_____

Today's Struggle:

_____

Small Victory Today:

_____

Where I Saw God Today:

_____

Prayer for Today:

_____

_____

_____

_____

_____

Reflect: Where have I seen small signs of God's presence this week?

_____

_____

_____

_____

_____

Chapter Reflection: How can I turn ordinary things into reminders of His goodness?

_____

_____

_____

_____

Journal

_____

_____

_____

_____

_____

_____

_____

_____

Doodle space:

Day 4 — Conversations with God

"And this is the confidence that we have toward him, that if we ask anything according to His will He hears us." 1 John 5:14

So, a bunch of my girlfriends are going to chuckle at this, but just as one of our friends bows her head to pray and declares, "I'm listening!" (Yes, Theresa, you made it into my book, and I never even mentioned you picking food off all our plates after saying "I'm not hungry!" LOL)

Sorry, I got off track.

Anyway, the point is: God is ALWAYS listening!

You do know that, right? He's there. He's listening ALL THE TIME! I say it's like having your friend on the phone and never hanging up. He is right there, hears you, knows what you're up to, and He WANTS you to talk to Him so He doesn't get bored. (Ok, so, I added that last part I'd get bored if I were on the other end of a call with you and you didn't talk to me! I'm sure God is far more patient than I am.)

"Hey, Kim, do you have to have some fancy prayer words and Bible verses handy in order to talk to Him?" Nope Just talk to Him like you're talking to a friend. Trust me, He's heard you talk your whole life...you think He hasn't heard you in your least Christian-like moments?

Answer: LOL

Got a problem? Tell Him.

Happy about something? Thank Him.

Amazed by something? Praise Him.

Worried? Give it to Him (then LEAVE it!). He knows everything already anyway! So, get it all off your chest and let it all go! Yeah, yeah... sounds easy, I know. It's not our nature to give it all up to God, it's our nature to sin.

You're thinking, "Kim, you're nuts, He didn't answer. This isn't a conversation. It's not a chat. It's one-sided."

Nope again. Quite the opposite. It's never a one-sided conversation with God.

My final thought for this episode: God answers ALL prayers... He just does it HIS way in HIS time... (ahem, that's what the "according to His Will" line in the Bible verse above was about!)

Oh, and I'm not going to add a prayer here because I want YOU to do the talking. I'll set you up, ready?

Sit in a quiet place, you can choose to close your eyes if you want, you can fold your hands if you want, but none of that is really necessary; it's how you prepare your heart that matters. So, relax and begin with the praise part. (Go back to the PAT episode)

Give God some loving'! Tell Him how awesome He is! Then ask Him for something... anything... patience, to take away anxiety, money to get through to the next payday. Finally, thank Him for all the incredible things He's done for you and for the world.

Too much? Ok, here's another approach: JUST START TALKING

Once you relinquish control to Him you will surely find peace! (Who said this? It's good!)

Anyway, let's break it down:

- Trust and Faith: Surrendering control is often linked to building trust in a higher power, believing that they have your best interests at heart. (You think He would've sent Jesus to die so gruesomely on the cross to save us from our own screw ups? He ALWAYS wants what's best for us!)
- Letting Go of Anxiety: When you relinquish control, you are essentially letting go of the anxieties and worries that often stem from trying to manage every situation. (Big Pharma won't like this part)
- Peace Beyond Understanding: The promise of peace often implies a sense of calm and serenity that transcends the anxieties of everyday life. (Love me a good benediction!)
- Divine Guidance: When you surrender yourself to God, you open yourself up to His Divine Guidance and support, allowing His omnipotence to shape your path. (He made EVERYTHING from scratch; you think He can't do miraculous things for you?)
- Finding Purpose: Surrendering can also be seen as a way to align your life with a greater purpose, finding meaning beyond your own personal desires. (Hmm, maybe I'll write a book)

Ok, moving on.

Let's try a prayer now:

Hey God (yup, He's ok with this),

Just checking in, although I know You've been here the whole time, probably belly laughing and face palming as I think I can run my world without You. Anyway, thanks for not hanging up.

Look, I've got stuff... you know, worries, joys, and a whole lot of mess. Help me hand it over to You and not grab it back five minutes later. Remind me that I don't need fancy words, just my heart.

Thanks for always listening to me, always loving me, and always showing up... even when I forget to.

Ok, gotta go, talk soon.

Amen.

"Pray continually." 1 Thessalonians 5:17

Today I'm Feeling:

_____

Today's Struggle:

_____

Small Victory Today:

_____

Where I Saw God Today:

_____

Prayer for Today:

_____

_____

_____

_____

_____

Reflect: When was the last time I talked to God like a friend instead of a formal speech?

_____

_____

_____

_____

_____

Chapter Reflection: How can I make prayer more personal, honest, and real?

_____

_____

_____

_____

_____

Journal

_____

_____

_____

_____

_____

_____

_____

_____

_____

Doodle space:

Day 5 — Putting the God in Godson

I was 41 before God allowed me to become a Godmother. Next to motherhood, it's the most important job I have. Have I failed both times? Oh, you bet.

Yet I am granted opportunity after opportunity to try again. Just as we are sinners who keep on sinning, forgiveness is there when we're ready to recognize and own up to our failure. God continues to give me chances to make things right with my kids as well as with my role as a Godmother.

Recently, my Godson reached out to me and seems to be going through something difficult. No details, but I don't need them. He didn't really want me, he wanted Jesus, and I am overjoyed that I could possibly bring them closer.

"Do you have that teen Bible that I gave you before you moved away?" I asked.

"No, I lost it in the move," he answered.

He didn't have access to a mobile device, so my suggestion of getting the Bible app was a moot point. I knew I needed to get him in the Word, but make it applicable, easy, and a blessing to him. I started digging around, looking for the best options.

Being a Lutheran since I was a baby, I love and always come right back to Luther's teachings and the Lutheran Study Bible. I wanted my Godson (baptized Lutheran at age 11 but not really having attended worship since) to have a good understanding of the simple concept that we are "saved by grace through faith" (Ephesians 2:8) and that "faith comes from hearing the Word" (Romans 10:17). I found myself ordering him Luther's Book of Prayer, the Small Catechism, and, most coveted by me for so long, the compact, soft cover, duotone Lutheran Study Bible.

I also sent him a couple of teen guy devotional books and a blank journal for writing his thoughts, prayers, hopes, and favorite verses.

The Bible I chose had to have a concordance. This is how I started diving into Scripture, even as a young woman. It helped me get through some of the toughest times in my life. I would think of a word, like HOPE, for example, and read every single verse about it. Some I would even write down and try to memorize. Words I've studied are love, forgiveness, patience, grace, courage, fear, and faith.

As I write this, I pray that, when he gets his package, he's not overwhelmed but blessed. I pray God sends His Holy Spirit to fill my dear Godson's heart with peace and faith, and to feed his hungry soul with the knowledge that he is so loved that, in order to show him His grace and mercy, God sent His son to die for him.

My friends, YOU are so loved!

YOU are forgiven!

YOU are saved!

...by grace, through your faith

Peace

> *"These commandments that I give you today are to be on your hearts... impress them on your children."*
> Deuteronomy 6:6-7

Today I'm Feeling:

_____

Today's Struggle:

_____

Small Victory Today:

_____

Where I Saw God Today:

_____

Prayer for Today:

_____

_____

_____

_____

_____

Reflect: What have I taught (or modeled) to those younger in faith or life?

_____

_____

_____

_____

Chapter Reflection: How is God using my influence in someone else's story?

_____

_____

_____

_____

_____

Journal

_____

_____

_____

_____

_____

_____

_____

_____

Doodle space:

Day 6 — What's Your Lenten Promise?

Many Christians, especially those with Roman Catholic backgrounds, keep the tradition of "giving up something for Lent". Some may give up chocolate, others something more behavioral, like watching TV. Whatever the "temptation", it's important to know why people give up such things.

If we look at what the Bible says about personal sacrifice during the 40- day season, we can start with Luke 9:23 which says:

> *And he said to all, "If anyone would come after me, let him deny himself and take up his cross daily and follow me.*

Jesus knew firsthand what it was like to "go without". He fasted several times in His life, even for 40 days before He was tempted. He never had the fanciest clothes or knew wealth. Though we are not commanded to fast, neither is it forbidden. Jesus actually mentions to His followers fasting after his death in Luke 5:35

> *"The days will come when the bridegroom is taken away from them, and then they will fast in those days."*

Although it's physically impossible for us to fast for 40 days like Jesus did (don't kid yourself, Jesus was only able to do this with the power of the Holy Spirit, remember, He was still a human), giving up something during this season will help us understand what Jesus went through as He willingly walked

Himself up the hill to die. We are to meditate and reflect upon His journey and, in the end, rejoice in his resurrection.

However, there's a catch. Making a Lenten promise should never be with the intention of trying to "look good" as a Christian. It should never be public, as to show righteousness to others. This is a personal promise made between you and God. It is to help you develop a closer relationship with Him and understanding of what He has done for us.

> *"And when you fast, do not look gloomy like the hypocrites, for they disfigure their faces that their fasting may be seen by others. Truly, I say to you, they have received their reward. But when you fast, anoint your head and wash your face, that your fasting may not be seen by others but by your Father who is in secret. And your Father who sees in secret will reward you. "Matthew 6:16-18*

So, what's your Lenten promise this year? Wait, don't tell me... you can keep that between the two of you... by the way, full disclosure, I fell back on my Lenten promise twice. I begged His forgiveness and moved forward, trusting in His mercy and grace!

Lord God, we thank You for your ultimate sacrifice on the cross which, in turn, gave us the ultimate reward. Help us to keep our focus on You and Your journey this Lenten season and always as we journey with You in our sacrifices, meditation and reflection. In Your name we humbly pray.

Amen

> *"Return to the Lord your God, for he is gracious and compassionate..."* Joel 2:13

Today I'm Feeling:

_____

Today's Struggle:

_____

Small Victory Today:

_____

Where I Saw God Today:

_____

Prayer for Today:

_____

_____

_____

_____

_____

Reflect: What have I let go of (or taken on) to grow closer to God this season?

_____

_____

_____

_____

Chapter Reflection: How does intentional sacrifice or devotion open up space for grace?

_____

_____

_____

_____

_____

Journal

_____

_____

_____

_____

_____

_____

_____

_____

_____

Doodle space:

Day 7 — Praise God That I Bear That Name

Let's be straight up with each other: I used to hesitate when it came to sharing my faith.

What would people think? Would they roll their eyes or hit that unfollow button? It was a challenge, but then I decided to take a leap of faith. I started sharing verses on Instagram, and before I knew it, I was blasting them out on Facebook too.

Now? I'm posting all the time, and honestly, I'm not looking back!

Have some friends unfollowed me? You bet! Have others unfriended me? Maybe... but honestly, I guess I'll never know (hmm, on second thought, maybe I WILL if they are "upstairs" one day... but were they truly friends?). What I do know is this: I'm proudly proclaiming the name of Jesus Christ, and that's what really matters!

In a world where faith often takes a backseat, it can be easy to feel embarrassed about our beliefs. As Lutherans, we're called to be bold.

Romans 1:16 says,

> *"For I am not ashamed of the gospel, for it is the power of God for salvation to everyone who believes..."*

That's right! We've got a gift of grace that deserves to be shared!

Let's not forget Jesus' words in Matthew 5:14-16:

"You are the light of the world. A city set on a hill cannot be hidden. Nor do people light a lamp and put it under a basket, but on a stand, and it gives light to all in the house. In the same way, let your light shine before others, so that they may see your good works and give glory to your Father who is in heaven."

Why would we hide our light? No way! Our faith is a beacon, and I want it shining bright for all to see!

So, now what? I share, I pray... not just for YOU reading this right now, but also for those who made me feel a bit ashamed. I pray that my posts bless you, and I hope those folks who unfollowed me find true peace and joy in Christ, our one true Savior.

Philippians 4:6-7 is my jam:

"do not be anxious about anything, but in everything by prayer and supplication with thanksgiving let your requests be made known to God. And the peace of God, which surpasses all understanding, will guard your hearts and your minds in Christ Jesus..."

Seriously, when we pray, we're inviting God into the mix. He can work wonders in their hearts—just like He's done in ours!

As we step out and share our faith, let's hold onto this verse found in 2 Timothy 1:7:

"for God gave us a spirit not of fear but of power and love and self-control."

Fear? Nah, not here!

We're filled with the Holy Spirit, and we've got the power to stand firm in our beliefs.

Let's embrace our identity as children of God, bearing His name with style and sass. Every post, every prayer, and every act of kindness can serve as a testimony to His love and grace. So go ahead—share that verse, spread that love, and let your light shine like the fabulous beacon you are!

Father, thank You for the gift of faith and for giving me the guts to share it boldly. Help me to be unashamed of the Gospel and to light up this world with Your love. I pray for those feeling distant from You because they need Your peace and joy. May our words and actions reflect Your grace and bring glory to Your name.

Amen.

> *"However, if you suffer as a Christian, do not be ashamed, but praise God that you bear that name."* 1 Peter 4:16

Today I'm Feeling:

_____

Today's Struggle:

_____

Small Victory Today:

_____

Where I Saw God Today:

_____

Prayer for Today:

_____

_____

_____

_____

_____

Reflect: What part of being a Christian feels hard — and how do I still choose joy?

_____

_____

_____

_____

Chapter Reflection: What does it mean to carry the name of Christ in how I live, speak, and love?

_____

_____

_____

_____

_____

Journal

_____

_____

_____

_____

_____

_____

_____

_____

Doodle space:

Weekly Reflection

What did I learn about God's presence in my every day this week?

_____

_____

_____

_____

_____

Where did I feel stretched in my faith?

_____

_____

_____

_____

_____

What surprised me about where God showed up?

_____

_____

_____

_____

_____

Biggest Growth Moment:

_____

_____

_____

_____

_____

Biggest Struggle:

_____

_____

_____

_____

_____

Where I Saw God Working:

_____

_____

_____

_____

_____

Bible Verse that Moved Me:

_____

_____

_____

_____

_____

What I'm Carrying into Next Week:

_____

_____

_____

_____

_____

10 Ways to Surrender Throughout the Week

☐ 1. Start the day with prayer instead of phone scrolling

☐ 2. Hand over one worry in prayer

☐ 3. Take a break when overwhelmed and invite God into the chaos

☐ 4. Speak kindly when it's hard

☐ 5. Let go of needing to be right

☐ 6. Say 'no' when it's the healthier choice

☐ 7. Trust God's timing — not your own

☐ 8. Ask for help

☐ 9. Extend grace to yourself

☐ 10. Praise God in the middle of a mess

Gratitude List

1._____

_____

2._____

_____

3._____

_____

4._____

_____

5._____

Weekly Memory Verse Challenge

Write this week's memory verse below. Decorate it. Doodle it. Memorize it. Make it yours!

Memory Verse:

_____

_____

_____

_____

_____

Doodle space:

Week 5

Mirror, Mirror— Reflection and Wisdom

No fairy tales here — just you, God, and a big ol' spiritual mirror. What have you learned so far? What needs to go, stay, or grow? This week we reflect with sass and soul. It's not about beating yourself up; it's about recognizing the wins, learning from the stumbles, and high fiving the Holy Spirit for carrying you this far.

Guided Prayer to Start the Week

Holy Spirit, hold the mirror steady. Help me see what You see — the growth, the grace, and even the grit. Show me the truth not to shame me, but to shape me into the woman You created me to be. Amen.

> *"If any of you lacks wisdom, you should ask God... and it will be given to you."* James 1:5

Day 1 — Pop Quiz

Salvation comes from...

a) works alone   *c) faith*

b) grace   *d) by grace through faith*

Go ahead, lock in your answer. (Don't worry, no one's grading—except maybe the Holy Spirit. No pressure.)

So, what did you pick?

Believe it or not, a lot of Christians think they know the answer. And honestly, many of us get a little fuzzy around this. Are we saved because we hand out tracts, go door-to door, teach Sunday School, or serve on every church committee?

Or are we saved because we simply believe—and receive?

Here's the truth, straight from Paul, who (let's be honest) didn't sugar coat a thing:

> *"So, faith comes from hearing, and hearing through the word of Christ."* Romans 10:17

And then he doubles down in Ephesians:

> *"For by grace you have been saved through faith. And this is not your own doing; it is the gift of God, not a result of works, so that no one may boast."* Ephesians 2:8–9

So, there it is: not by works. Not by hustle. Not by trying to earn your spot at the table. It's by grace. Through faith. Full stop.

God didn't create a to-do list for salvation—He offered a gift. And when we say yes to that gift, when we put our faith in His grace and mercy, something amazing happens: the works we do stop being about earning His love and start being about sharing His love. They become fruit, not currency.

So, if you answered "d" —ding ding ding! You got it.

Let's not just leave it at head knowledge. Let it sink in today: you are saved not because of what you do, but because of what Jesus already did.

Walk in that. Rest in that. And let your life reflect it—not to prove your worth, but to reflect His glory.

Now go shine a little of that grace today. And maybe celebrate with a little pie. (Lemon meringue, anyone?)

Pray this:

Lord, you are the light of the world! Thank you for Your gift of abounding grace! Help me to shine your light so others may believe and receive everlasting life with You. In Jesus' name, Amen

> *"Let us examine our ways and test them and let us return to the Lord." Lamentations 3:40*

Today I'm Feeling:

_____

Today's Struggle:

_____

Small Victory Today:

_____

Where I Saw God Today:

_____

Prayer for Today:

_____

_____

_____

_____

_____

Reflect: What parts of my heart or habits are being tested right now?

_____

_____

_____

_____

Chapter Reflection: How can I approach trials as opportunities for soul-growth?

_____

_____

_____

_____

_____

Journal

_____

_____

_____

_____

_____

_____

_____

_____

_____

_____

_____

_____

_____

_____

Doodle space:

Day 2 — Double Standard?

Why do we hurt the ones we love the most?

Why is it that I can spend my day with adolescents who have major behavior and attitude problems and treat them in a calm, loving, respectful manner, yet when I get home to my family, I can be nasty and impatient? Why the Dr. Jekyll and Mr. Hyde?

There are students who have told me "where to go" and, with the start of the next school day, I forgive them and wipe the slate clean. I never hold grudges with my students. However, I can go days without speaking to my husband because of a disagreement or misunderstanding. I hold past behaviors over my daughter's head if she (has the nerve to – Lol) ask me for something. Why is it so difficult to let go of things when dealing with family?

As I write this it's Ash Wednesday, the start of the Lenten season. The next 40 days will be a time of reflection on one's own sinful life and the ultimate sacrifice Christ made to wipe the slate clean. If He can, I can.

No, I must. What an amazing expression of how much He loves us! So, today, I have decided what I'm giving up for Lent and, with practice, forever:

I will not treat my family with disrespect. I will show them how much I love them with not only my words, but my actions. I will speak kindly and calmly; I will not be selfish or authoritative.

Sure, I could give up something common like chocolate or ice. cream. Where's the sacrifice? What will it prove or change? My personal sacrifice needs to be something that will change my behavior and honor God. It should force me to think about how I love my family and friends, and above all, how Jesus loved me to the extent that He gave His life for me.

"First take the plank out of your own eye..." Matthew 7:5

Today I'm Feeling:

_____

Today's Struggle:

_____

Small Victory Today:

_____

Where I Saw God Today:

_____

Prayer for Today:

_____

_____

_____

_____

_____

Reflect: Where have I judged someone unfairly or held them to a different standard than myself?

_____

_____

_____

_____

_____

Chapter Reflection: What does grace look like when I give it, not just receive it?

_____

_____

_____

_____

_____

Journal

_____

_____

_____

_____

_____

_____

_____

_____

_____

_____

Doodle space:

Day 3 — A Nice Way to End a Great Week...

Here I sit, waiting for the start of my daughter's handbell festival. It's a concert performed by an amassed bell choir of eight different churches, some of which have more than one bell choir. There are approximately 75+ ringers playing. It's absolutely breathtaking. My daughter is the tiniest ringer here. It's her second year in the bell choir and her second year at this festival.

She is my favorite musician right now...

I love watching her play. She has beautiful technique, and she does have a great teacher. Mrs. Stahl has known Sara since kindergarten and has watched her grow and change. Now my little musician sings in the choir, plays handbells and plays flute in the band.

I do wish her flute playing would continue to improve, but I'm afraid she is losing her interest. However, from the very first day she brought home that instrument, she has produced perfect notes. Am I wrong to push her to continue? I try to praise her musical ability whenever I can, but she still lets out a little moan if I suggest that she practice. I want to encourage her, not exhaust her. I don't want to demand perfection, but I do want her to understand the value of growing her gifts. It's a fine line—one many parents walk. I know what I would have done with my own musical journey if I'd had more urging. I sometimes wonder: *am I doing the right things to encourage hers?*

Proverbs 22:6 reminds us, *"Train up a child in the way he should go, even when he is old he will not depart from it."*

I try to hold that close. I know she won't remember every note she's played or every time I asked her to practice—but I hope she remembers that I believed in her. That I saw something special and wanted to help her grow it.

> *"Every good and perfect gift is from above."* James 1:17

I see those gifts in her every time she picks up a bell, sings a song, or breathes life into her flute. And I'm reminded how good God is to let me witness it. Maybe tonight I'll tell her how proud I am. Not just for the music she plays, but for the joy and light she brings when she does it. That, more than anything, is a gift worth celebrating.

> *"You make known to me the path of life; you will fill me with joy in your presence..."* Psalm 16:11

Today I'm Feeling:

_____

Today's Struggle:

_____

Small Victory Today:

_____

Where I Saw God Today:

_____

Prayer for Today:

_____

_____

_____

_____

Reflect: How has God shown up for me this week?

_____

_____

_____

_____

Chapter Reflection: What wins or joys do I need to pause and celebrate before moving on?

_____

_____

_____

_____

Journal

_____

_____

_____

_____

_____

_____

_____

_____

_____

_____

Doodle space:

Day 4 — Fashion Fads, Flying Boxers...

If I have to tell one more kid to pull up his pants, I might just nail a 95th complaint to the school office door. Seriously, what is happening out there?

Why in the world would a young girl get a tattoo on her neck?

How wide are those things in his ears? Is that a dinnerplate or an earring? What gauge is that — Hula Hoop Size?

Sometimes I feel like I fell asleep during the normal fashion trends and woke up in some dystopian circus. <<shudder>>

I get it: Times change, people change, styles change. Luther himself would probably make a cringe face at some of the things we get hung up on. (He wasn't exactly the poster child for polished appearances either. Homeboy loved his "bier".)

But some things aren't just about style — they're about wisdom, vocation, and respecting the body God entrusted to us.

> *"So, whether you eat or drink, or whatever you do, do all for the glory of God."*1 Corinthians 10:31

Spoiler alert: Glorifying God probably doesn't involve advertising your boxer briefs to your math teacher.

Back in the day — early 90s — the sagging pants parade got you a suspension faster than you could say "belt." Now? It's everywhere. I hate to be the Pants Police, but when a student's boxers are on display like a booty billboard, what am I supposed to do?

Inevitably the student blasts, "Why are you looking!?" I want to say, "Because, honey, you're walking around with a flashing, neon sign on your @$$."

<<shudder>>

Tattoos.

I have six. (Sorry, Grandpa. He said [about piercings], "If God meant you to have holes in your ears, you would have been born with them," and I still pushed my luck.)

Here's the difference: I got them as an adult, after establishing my career, and they're placed respectfully, where I can cover them if needed.

These poor girls today...They don't seem to think past Saturday night.

What job are you going to land with a giant neck tattoo? What's that scripture again?

> *"Or do you not know that your body is a temple of the Holy Spirit within you, whom you have from God? You are not your own, for you were bought with a price. So, glorify God in your body."* 1 Corinthians 6:19–20

Yeah. That.

While we're at it — just wait till pregnancy and gravity team up on those tattoos climbing up your sides, ladies. Spoiler alert for the girls: it's not going to be pretty. I suspect the plastic surgeons are already rubbing their hands together in gleeful anticipation of all that future tattoo removal business.

Meanwhile, these poor kids are tattooing frogs, flames, the symbol for Combination 21 on the Chinese restaurant takeout menu, and who knows-what-else on their necks, sides, and backs before they even open a savings account. Someone should gently remind them to reread the above verse from 1 Corinthians. *Your body is a temple, not a billboard for bad decisions.*

Let's have a little chat about gauges. We're talking about earlobes stretched so wide you could practically pass the church offering plate through them.

One of my students had "plugs" that look like wine bottle corks the size of silver dollars. When he pulls those out someday, it's not going to snap back into place, my dear.

Think melting candle wax.

<<shudder>>

I understand — times change, society shifts.

God gives us free will, sure. Christian freedom is not license to do whatever feels good at the moment. It's the freedom to serve, to honor, to reflect Christ.

> *"'All things are lawful,' but not all things are helpful. 'All things are lawful,' but not all things build up."* 1 Corinthians 10:23

Luther famously said, "Sin boldly, but believe more boldly still."

Meaning?

Yes, you're going to make mistakes.

Yes, you might have to live with some questionable choices (and saggy tattoos). But Jesus doesn't love us because we look polished and perfect. He loves us because He is good, not because we are. He invites us — messy, tattooed, pierced, sagging pants and all — to cling to Him harder than we cling to any trend or image.

> *"For freedom Christ has set us free; stand firm therefore, and do not submit again to a yoke of slavery."* Galatians 5:1

So, I'll keep loving these kids.

I'll keep laughing and cringing and <<shudder>>ing.

I'll keep pointing others to the kind of freedom that doesn't wear out, stretch out, or fade. The kind that was bought for them — and for me — by blood, mercy, unrelenting grace, and a God who sees past the sagging jeans and stretched-out ears... straight into the heart.

> *"People look at the outward appearance, but the Lord looks at the heart."* 1 Samuel 16:7

Today I'm Feeling:

_____

Today's Struggle:

_____

Small Victory Today:

_____

Where I Saw God Today:

_____

Prayer for Today:

_____

_____

_____

_____

_____

Reflect: Where am I more focused on image than integrity?

_____

_____

_____

_____

_____

Chapter Reflection: How is God reshaping what I value — in myself and others?

_____

_____

_____

_____

_____

Journal

_____

_____

_____

_____

_____

_____

_____

_____

_____

Doodle space:

Day 5 — 10 Random Facts About Me

I found this blog post idea from a web search. Part of me wonders whether you will even care about this, but I have this crazy urge to write something interesting... It'll be interesting to *me*... I'm just counting on you finding it interesting (dare I say amusing?)!

> 1. I have to clean my ears with a Q-Tip after I shower. It's now a habit and, if I don't do it, I feel totally uncomfortable for the rest of the day. (TMI? Oh well... you already read it... move along))

> 2. I still have my teddy bear that I got for my Christening. He's sitting by my bed on my nightstand, all worn and messed up. His original mouth is missing (from when my dog Chester chewed him), his nose is half off, his left ear is split and both ears are pierced. (Don't ask, it was the 70s & 80s) He wears a cream-colored dickie-looking thing that I knitted when I was about 10. It's about 3" x 4" because that's about the size of my attention span. I once left Teddy outside and it rained; I cried as though I had killed him or something. Oh, if that bear could talk!

> 3. I am Type A and have OCD. I have a specific routine in the morning and, if I deviate from it, my whole day is messed up. Also, there's this weird thing I do while riding in a car: ever since I was little, when driving past a light pole, street sign, or bridge, I move my elbow in and out as if to miss hitting it as I go by. I used to duck

when going under over passes, but I'm a big girl now and stopped.

4. I have synesthesia: I associate colors with numbers and vice versa. Red is 3, blue is 4, yellow is 9. Don't ask, I even think it's weird... Look it up. It's a thing.

5. I have an insatiable appetite for electronic gadgets. I love to have the latest and greatest, though finances don't always allow it! I love my Bluetooth gadgets, my computers, the interactive board at work. I had an original Nintendo Game Boy (so did my mom!).

6. I hate to eat raw onion, raw peppers, raw broccoli, raw spinach, beets and cauliflower... but I absolutely LOVE creamed spinach, lima beans, steamed broccoli, raw string beans, and cooking with onions! I'm still waiting to "grow out of hating the onions thing" that everyone told me would happen.

7. Without knowing how to ski, and while staying in a slope-side condo, I skied down a black diamond in order to get to the lodge to buy my lift ticket and lesson package.

8. My perfect salad: green, romaine lettuce, tomato, cucumber, chopped egg, bacon, grilled chicken, shredded cheddar, dried cranberries, walnuts... ranch dressing

9. In 1978 I had a great collection of Topps baseball cards and a full set of Yankees. I loved to flip cards with the boys in school; I would bring in a small stack, include a few of my good doubles (like Bucky Dent, Thurman Munson, Catfish Hunter, Reggie Jackson)

and come home with at least double the stack and more awesome cards. Boys feared me, but they continued to challenge my amazing card-flipping ability... I know, it was all luck-of-the-draw (flip?)!

10. Mom taught me that I should always reconcile the register receipt from the grocery store with all the purchases once we got home. She would call out the item and price, I would cross it off with pencil.

Sometimes we would catch an error and get a few bucks back! One day while in high school I was at a friend's house and, upon returning from a trip to the grocery store with her mom, I started freaking out that everyone just started putting things away without telling me the prices!

I realized then that it was NOT a thing everyone does. We had a good chuckle about it, though! I still check my receipts.

There you have it. I wonder if this post should have been entitled "10 Things That Make Me Weird?" Some of the things I've mentioned are pretty normal to me, though.

Okay, so what does God think about me spilling my guts about Q-tips and my messed-up Teddy? Well, He made me this way, right? And God doesn't make mistakes.

Psalm 139:14 says I'm "fearfully and wonderfully made" – even the weird parts! Being honest about my quirks? Seems better than pretending I'm some perfect Stepford wife. Plus, life's full of funny, little things, and God's in all of it, even my bizarre car elbow thing (Again, do NOT judge).

If me sharing my oddness makes someone else feel a little less weird, that's a good thing, right? We're all in this crazy human thing together. Get your weirdness on!

So, yeah, I'm gonna keep it real. God made me this slightly strange, but hopefully interesting, person. Deal with it. All I have to do in this life is to honor Him and do all things to His Glory!

> *"I praise you because I am fearfully and wonderfully made..."* Psalm 139:14

Today I'm Feeling:

_____

Today's Struggle:

_____

Small Victory Today:

_____

Where I Saw God Today:

_____

Prayer for Today:

_____

_____

_____

_____

Reflect: What unique qualities has God given me — and do I celebrate them?

_____

_____

_____

_____

Chapter Reflection: Where do I need to embrace my own God-given weirdness with pride?

_____

_____

_____

_____

Journal

_____

_____

_____

_____

_____

_____

_____

_____

_____

_____

_____

_____

Doodle space:

Day 6 — Things That Make Me Happy

So, I've had this one idea to write about: talk about my pet-peeves. Though I still might write that one (kinda negative, right?), I'm feeling more happy and less ornery today. So, I thought I'd write a happy one.

Things that make me happy... here are some:

1. Seeing my girls sleeping. OK, let me just say that it's NOT because they are quiet and not aggravating me (all the time), but when they are asleep, they are so beautiful and peaceful. I could stare at them forever.

Is it weird that I have more than a few pictures of them sleeping? Don't answer that.

2. Flowers. Today, and over the last couple of weeks, Sara and I planted lots of colorful, pretty flowers. I actually planted perennial bulbs, too, which will give me recurring happiness year after year! (If I didn't plant them upside down... I do NOT have a green thumb!) Flowers come in so many pretty colors, it's hard not to smile when I look at them.

3. Bela's laugh. Since she was little, she just has the best belly laugh ever. When she's not Sleeping Beauty or hangry (often both), but oh, I love to hear that laugh!

4. Technology (gadgets!). I have always loved my electronics. I love to wire up the satellite, TV, stereo, surround sound, computer and its peripherals... everything! When I got my first smartphone years ago, I was in my glory all over again. How did I survive

without this little miracle before now? Oh, and technology in the classroom is a total game-changer.

5. Confession/Absolution. One of my two favorite parts of the church service. I get such a wonderful, overwhelming feeling of happiness when Pastor tells me that I'm forgiven. Chills and amazing grace!

6. The Benediction. My other favorite part of the service. No, not because the service is almost over (be nice - if you like when the church service is over, then you clearly aren't at the right church), but it's the nicest feeling when I get blessed. I feel like I've been refreshed and ready to go out in the world!

7. Payday. Duh. All praise and glory to God!

8. The beach. I can't imagine living inland and land locked. I love the ocean, the beach, and boating so much. It was always a part of my life growing up and it all just makes me so happy and relaxed. If I have a rough day, I head to the beach or the docks. If I have a little extra time before having to be somewhere and I'm happy? I go there then, too. "Down the docks" is the perfect place for me to pray for comfort, strength, and peace, as well as to give thanks for joy and all the amazing gifts He gives us, like grace mercy, and all things marine.

9. Sitting by the campfire or firepit. Again, like the beach, it's so relaxing. I prefer the campfire because, at home, I'm always thinking about what I SHOULD be doing, like cleaning or laundry. While camping, even if we're a half-hour away, I feel so disconnected from

reality. Of course, it only lasts a couple of days, but I'll take it!

10. Music. Like the beach, music has been a major part of my life since childhood. I love all types of music: classical, reggae, jazz, rock, country, soul, rap, showtunes, and blues. Music comes in so many forms, so it's easy to match it up with however you're feeling. Some songs even represent eras of our lives and can bring back a certain memory! How wonderful!

So, there you have it: some of the things that make me happy. What makes me even happier than any of these is enjoying them with those I love! That's the ultimate...

Be happy and be well...

> *"...whatever is true, whatever is noble... think about such things."* Philippians 4:8

I pray: thank you, Father.

Today I'm Feeling:

_____

Today's Struggle:

_____

Small Victory Today:

_____

Where I Saw God Today:

_____

Prayer for Today:

_____

_____

_____

_____

_____

Reflect: What little joys ground me when life gets chaotic?

_____

_____

_____

_____

_____

Chapter Reflection: How can noticing the good keep me anchored in gratitude?

_____

_____

_____

_____

_____

Journal

_____

_____

_____

_____

_____

_____

_____

_____

_____

Doodle space:

Day 7 — Evidence...

Apparently, there are people in the world who, surprisingly, do not believe in God. (Huh? Say what now?) Yet, if we simply look around a bit, we see evidence of His existence everywhere, every day. Whether or not you are a believer (or maybe you'll find yourself talking with someone questioning their belief), here are just a few to get one thinking:

> 1. Babies - two microscopic cells, completely different from each other, come together to immediately begin a new life. Cells divide, grow, change, and eventually create bone, muscle, organs, blood vessels. A heart appears and beats rhythmically at around day 22! A brain forms and controls involuntary processes of that new creation: the human body. That brain acquires, stores and uses knowledge about language, math, and relationships. A mother's body provides everything the baby needs, even at her own expense. A baby is born, with fingers, toes, eyelashes, eyebrows, hundreds of bones, a personality, a future, a plan. The miracle continues as this baby grows into a child, adult, and eventually reaches the end of life.

> God knew exactly what He was doing when He made us. No cosmic explosion or amount of evolution could ever produce such a beautiful thing. Which leads me to...

> 2. Galaxies and the universe - perhaps there WAS a cosmic explosion, though I'll never know. I wasn't there. (Wait, I suppose I WILL find out when I get to

Heaven, right? Cool. Ok, moving on. Sorry for getting distracted.) I DO know that there exists an omnipotent god who created an infinite variety of beautiful planets, all with their own unique atmospheres, belonging to and revolving around brilliant, powerful orbs of energy. There may very well be varied life forms throughout our vast universe as well. The very thought that there is no way to measure the infinity that is "space" that could only be created by our awesome and awe-inspiring God is EVIDENCE!

3. Life, in general - remember learning about and comparing animal cells and plant cells in science class? There are similarities and differences, but both are alive, created to support each other, to co-exist, to reproduce, to evolve. Plants and their pollination, transpiration, and continued germination all contribute to producing oxygen which is necessary for animal life. Each species of animal, whether herbivore, carnivore or omnivore, contributes to and exists in balance with each other as well as plant life to continue a beautiful, complex and miraculous cycle. Still need more?

4. Love - we receive, we give, we feel, we show. It's relative, though. There is agape, philos, and eros, of which I wrote back in a separate musing. Some people are privileged to experience all forms, the most freely given and shown is agape from our Heavenly Father. It is the same love Christ had for us when He died for us, and the one that we will least comprehend. Agape refers to God's unconditional, selfless, and sacrificial love for humanity, as demonstrated in Jesus Christ's

death on the cross. It's a love that is not based on works or whether we are able to reciprocate it, but is freely given and extends to all people, even those who are not worthy. Philos is the love that we share in communion with one another as His children. The dictionary defines it as this: a friend, to be friendly to one, wish him well, a friend, an associate he who associates familiarly with one, a companion. It's what allows us to be compassionate and empathetic, helping others in need. Another "earthly" love is Eros, which is what draws two people together in their desire for intimacy.

It is fully intended by Our Creator to be shared physically within the context of marriage. Not one person experiences love in the same manner, but when ANY form of love exists and is felt, there also exists further evidence.

Babies, galaxies, life and love... All beautiful, inexplicable evidence of our omnipotent, omniscient and omnipresent God. Seriously, try explaining everything I've mentioned above without a God who's got it all figured out – His power, His smarts, and His being everywhere. It's like Psalm 19:1 shouts from the rooftops (or, even more accurately, the vastness of space):

> *"The heavens declare the glory of God, and the sky above proclaims His handiwork."*

You know my homeboy Luther? He was pretty sharp on this stuff. He'd look at a flower or a newborn and be like, "See? That's God's doing!" He wasn't just about the Bible (though he really was all about the Bible!), but he saw God's fingerprints all over creation. It's like God's leaving little "I was here" notes for us to find. Ponder that today.

"Examine yourselves to see whether you are in the faith; test yourselves." 2 Corinthians 13:5

Today I'm Feeling:

_____

Today's Struggle:

_____

Small Victory Today:

_____

Where I Saw God Today:

_____

Prayer for Today:

_____

_____

_____

_____

_____

Reflect: What fruit or evidence of faith is growing in my life right now?

_____

_____

_____

_____

_____

Chapter Reflection: What area is still a struggle — and where have I clearly grown?

_____

_____

_____

_____

_____

_____

Journal

_____

_____

_____

_____

_____

_____

_____

_____

_____

Weekly Reflection

What wisdom have I gained from the journey so far?

_____

_____

_____

_____

_____

Where have I seen real growth or breakthrough?

_____

_____

_____

_____

_____

What old thoughts or lies have I let go of?

_____

_____

_____

_____

_____

Biggest Growth Moment:

_____

_____

_____

_____

Biggest Struggle:

_____

_____

_____

_____

_____

Where I Saw God Working:

_____

_____

_____

_____

_____

Bible Verse that Moved Me:

_____

_____

_____

_____

_____

What I'm Carrying into Next Week:

_____

_____

_____

_____

_____

10 Ways to Surrender Throughout the Week

☐ 1. Start the day with prayer instead of phone scrolling

☐ 2. Hand over one worry in prayer

☐ 3. Take a break when overwhelmed and invite God into the chaos

☐ 4. Speak kindly when it's hard

☐ 5. Let go of needing to be right

☐ 6. Say 'no' when it's the healthier choice

☐ 7. Trust God's timing — not your own

☐ 8. Ask for help

☐ 9. Extend grace to yourself

☐ 10. Praise God in the middle of a mess

Gratitude List

1._____

_____

2._____

_____

3._____

_____

4._____

_____

5._____

_____

Weekly Memory Verse Challenge

Write this week's memory verse below. Decorate it. Doodle it. Memorize it. Make it yours!

Memory Verse:

_____

_____

_____

_____

_____

_____

Doodle space:

Week 6

Still Standing— God's Faithfulness in Every Season

Sis, look at you — still here, still fighting, still showing up. God's track record? Flawless. Even when we've been flaky, faithless, or full-on facedown, He's stayed steady. This week is your reminder that His promises don't expire, His grace doesn't run out, and His presence never packs up and leaves. You've made it this far for a reason.

Guided Prayer to Start the Week

God, thank You for staying when I wandered, for holding me when I doubted, and for carrying me when I collapsed. You are the reason I'm still standing. Remind me of Your faithfulness every single day. Amen.

> *"But those who hope in the Lord will renew their strength..."* Isaiah 40:31

Day 1 — Take Not Thy Holy Spirit from Me

"If you love me, you will keep my commandments. And I will ask the Father, and he will give you another Helper, to be with you forever, even the Spirit of truth, whom the world cannot receive, because it neither sees him nor knows him.

> *"You know him, for he dwells with you and will be in you."* John 14:15-17

David's cry in Psalm 51 always gets me. *"Take not Your Holy Spirit from me."* That line? It's not just a plea for forgiveness - it's desperation for presence. It's the voice of someone who's tasted closeness with God... and is terrified of losing it.

Yeah. I've been there. You?

There was a stretch not too long ago when I felt like I was walking through molasses, spiritually, mentally, emotionally. I was anxious, foggy, unable to focus. Sundays were the hardest. I'd show up, sit in the pew, and just stare. People around me were worshiping, praying, singing... and I was barely hanging on. Not praying. Not connecting. Just going through the motions with a heart that felt disconnected from everything that mattered.

And the worst part? I knew it. I knew I was drifting. The enemy was whispering all the usual lies, and I was letting him. It wasn't one big crisis—it was just that slow fade. That numbness. That ache of knowing you're not okay but not sure how to get back.

Then one morning, it all caught up with me. During worship, I finally broke. Head bowed, heart racing, hands clenched - I prayed the only thing I could think to say:

"Father God, please help me. Fill me with Your Holy Spirit. I need You. I can't do this without You."

And you know what? He met me there. Not in fireworks and flashing lights—but in quiet tears, goosebumps, and peace that didn't make sense. It wasn't that the Holy Spirit had gone anywhere. I had just stopped paying attention. All I had to do was ask. The Holy Spirit isn't some bonus feature of faith—He is God. And He's not just showing up in the happiest moments or major life decisions.

He's there in the middle of your Monday. He's working through the Word, through the Sacraments, and even through your overwhelmed heart when your brain is already halfway into next Tuesday's grocery list.

As Lutherans, we know the Spirit's job isn't to make us feel spiritual - it's to call, gather, enlighten, and sanctify the whole Church. That includes you. That includes me. Whether we're on fire for the Lord or barely flickering, He is always at work.

These days, I try to ask for His help before things unravel. Not just when I'm desperate, but when things are fine. In the quiet, the ordinary, and yes—when I'm about to snap over laundry and dinner plans.

He fills. He comforts. He guides. Every time. Because of the Holy Spirit, I am not alone.

I am not forgotten. I am loved.

I say to Him:

God,

Thank You for staying close—even when I don't. I'm sorry for the times I try to run this life on my own. Please fill me again. Right now. Calm my chaos. Focus my thoughts. Center my heart on Christ. Remind me that You're not only with me in the hard moments, but in the quiet, unseen ones too.

Be my Comforter, my Helper, and the peace I didn't know I needed.

In Jesus' name, Amen.

"And I will ask the Father, and he will give you another advocate... the Spirit of truth." John 14:16-17

Today I'm Feeling:

_____

Today's Struggle:

_____

Small Victory Today:

_____

Where I Saw God Today:

_____

Prayer for Today:

_____

_____

_____

_____

Reflect: When have I felt distant from the Holy Spirit — and what drew me back?

_____

_____

_____

_____

_____

Chapter Reflection: How can I create space for the Spirit to move freely in my life?

_____

_____

_____

_____

_____

_____

_____

Journal

_____

_____

_____

_____

_____

_____

_____

_____

_____

Doodle space:

Day 2 — Cast Me Not Away

David's cry in Psalm 51 hits hard: *"Cast me not away from Your presence..."* Psalm 51:11a

He is wrecked. Spiritually gutted. He's looking at the heap of sin in his life—adultery, deception, murder—and he's not just ashamed. He's afraid. Afraid that maybe this time he's gone too far. That maybe God has had enough.

Haven't we all been there in some form or another?

This line in the psalm is more than a poetic plea. It's the desperate cry of a man who knows exactly what separation from God could mean. David is begging not just for forgiveness, but for presence. To David (and face it, to us), to be cast away from God's presence is, simply put, the worst thing that could ever happen. I can barely wrap my brain around that, but as I try to, the utter despair I feel is overwhelming.

And yet... David knew something deeper. He knew that God is faithful. He even taught that truth to his son Solomon:

> *"...If you seek him, he will be found by you, but if you forsake him, he will cast you off forever."* 1 Chronicles 28:9

That sounds a little harsh—until you realize David's not speaking from theory. He's lived it. He's felt the crushing weight of sin, the ache of guilt, and the sweetness of mercy. He knew firsthand that God searches hearts and welcomes repentance.

So, here's the good news: our God is not in the business of ghosting His children. He isn't sitting in heaven keeping a tally of screw-ups so He can finally cut us loose. That's not how grace works. Not in David's time, and not now.

> *"...Be strong and courageous and do it. Do not be afraid and do not be dismayed, for the Lord God, even my God, is with you. He will not leave you or forsake you..."* 1 Chronicles 28:20

Let's not forget the story Jesus tells in Luke 15 about the prodigal son. That kid had one foot in the pigpen and the other practically in hell, but when he turned back, his father RAN to him. That's what our Heavenly Father does too—He runs to us, throws His arms around us, and welcomes us back.

> *"For this my son was dead and is alive again; he was lost and is found."* Luke 15:24

That's the heart of God. He never casts us away when we come to Him in true repentance. Never.

We're all prodigals in some way—some more dramatic than others, sure—but all of us sin, wander, mess up. Every time we come crawling back with a broken and contrite heart, God is there. Not with shame, but with celebration.

So, if your heart's been feeling heavy...

If you've been wondering whether God's tired of your repeated confessions... If you've questioned whether you've wandered too far...

Take a breath. He's still here. He's not casting you away. Not now. Not ever.

Now pray with me:

Dear Lord,

Thank You for never turning Your back on me. Even when I mess up - again and again—You don't cast me away. You wait for me. You pursue me. You welcome me with open arms every time I return to You in repentance. Give me a heart that never stops seeking Your presence and a spirit that clings to Your faithfulness.

Help me to trust in Your promises and rest in Your grace.

In Jesus' name again I pray,

> *"Do not cast me from your presence or take your Holy Spirit from me."* Psalm 51:11

Amen

Today I'm Feeling:

_____

Today's Struggle:

_____

Small Victory Today:

_____

Where I Saw God Today:

_____

Prayer for Today:

_____

_____

_____

_____

Reflect: What fear or shame has made me feel far from God?

_____

_____

_____

_____

Chapter Reflection: How does grace pull me back to the presence I never truly left?

_____

_____

_____

_____

Journal

_____

_____

_____

_____

_____

_____

_____

_____

_____

Doodle space:

Day 3 — Renew My Spirit

We are born into sin. That was a tough pill to swallow especially when I became a mom. I remember looking at my brand-new baby girl, all snuggly and pink, while thinking there is no way this child is a sinner. I mean, she could barely lift her own head. However, as I grew in faith, I came to understand what David already knew when he wrote Psalm 51, that we don't start clean and then mess it up—we're born with the mess.

Sin isn't something we learn, it's something we inherit.

That's why we cling to Baptism.

While we are born into sin, we are also born again through water and the Word. In my Lutheran understanding, Baptism isn't just a symbolic act. It's God's work. His promise. It's where we are made new —actually, spiritually, eternally new.

> "he saved us, not because of works done by us in righteousness, but according to his own mercy, by the washing of regeneration and renewal of the Holy Spirit," Titus 3:5

That's what David's asking for in Psalm 51. A clean heart, yes—but also a renewed spirit. A fresh start. A holy reboot. I don't know about you, but I could use one of those daily.

The word "renew" literally means to make new again. That implies it once was new—once clean, pure, God-pleasing. But life (and sin) has a way of wearing us down, don't they? The spiritual grime builds up. Our spirits get distracted, discouraged, defeated. We start living by feelings instead of faith, by emotion instead of truth.

Yet through His mercy, God restores us.

That's the beauty of this psalm. David isn't making excuses. He's not asking for a quick fix or a spiritual band-aid. He's pleading for transformation. We can ask for the same.

No matter how many times I mess it up—and oh boy, do I — God is faithful to renew. He fills me again with His Spirit, strengthens my faith, and reminds me who I am: a baptized child of God. A sinner, yes —but also a saint.

So, like David, I'm praying: Renew my spirit, Lord.

Make me new - again.

Heavenly Father,

Thank You for washing me clean in the waters of Baptism and giving me new life through Your Holy Spirit. I come to You today, aware of my sin, and in desperate need of Your mercy. Renew my spirit. Restore my joy. Remind me daily that I am Yours – redeemed, forgiven, and loved. Help me live as Your child, not by my own strength, but through the Spirit You so graciously give.

In Jesus' name I pray,

Amen.

Today I'm Feeling:

_____

Today's Struggle:

_____

Small Victory Today:

_____

Where I Saw God Today:

_____

Prayer for Today:

_____

_____

_____

_____

_____

Reflect: What part of me needs renewal right now?

_____

_____

_____

_____

_____

Chapter Reflection: How does the Spirit bring freshness and life where I feel dry?

_____

_____

_____

_____

_____

Journal

_____

_____

_____

_____

_____

Doodle space:

Day 4 — Restore My Joy

It was a long time ago that I decided to write about Psalm 51 and David's cry for mercy.

He was SO bogged down by his sinfulness, the only way was UP (and, after sending his repentant heart to the Father, pun is FULLY intended... "up", get it? Heaven? Whatever, keep reading).

This chapter is filled with The Word because God has sent TONS of promises of JOY. The only thing is, He never said it would come easily.

> *"Count it all joy, my brothers, when you meet trials of various kinds, for you know that the testing of your faith produces steadfastness."* James 1:2-3

So, here, in James, God tells us we will find joy in our trials? Huh? Keep reading. When we face tough times, we cry out to the Father and He helps us up. Stay the course, keep praying and maintain focus on Christ.

Your faith will carry you and you will persevere! Piece of cake, right? Ha!

Good thing God gave us Plan B:

> *"And the angel said to them, 'Fear not, for behold, I bring you good news of great joy that will be for all the people. For unto you is born this day in the city of David a Savior, who is Christ the Lord.'"* Luke 2:10-11

Listen, your Heavenly Father knows you better than you know yourself. He KNOWS earthly living is sometimes difficult! That's why He sent us Jesus! That's called GRACE. We have a Savior to give us HOPE of an eternity with Him in Glory... All that's required is our FAITH! His Grace covers it all. The joy in knowing that gave us some rules...and it's pretty simple:

> *"If you keep my commandments, you will abide in my love, just as I have kept my Father's commandments and abide in his love. These things I have spoken to you, that my joy may be in you, and that your joy may be full."* John 15:10-12

"... that my joy may be in you, and that your joy may be full" Wow. Love God, love others, do the right thing... and we are rewarded with being filled with His Joy! Wait! If you act now, He'll throw in this BONUS FOR FREE: the fulfillment of His promises... we just need to ask, and He will give us what we need! (spoken in my best TV pitch guy voice)

> [Jesus said] *"In that day you will ask nothing of me. Truly, truly, I say to you, whatever you ask of the Father in my name, he will give it to you. Until now you have asked nothing in my name. Ask, and you will receive, that your joy may be full."* (John 16:23-24)

Look, this life is not always going to be easy. We will face trials until the day we go home to Glory. The real trial is keeping our faith in Him and knowing in our hearts that He'll sustain us. David finally figured it out and, through his faith and a truly repentant heart, was saved by God's amazing grace. David, the poster child for sin, and whose joy WAS indeed restored, mapped out for us the way to PURE JOY THROUGH TRIALS.

We simply need to have faith that our gracious Father will sustain us.

> *"May the God of hope fill you with all joy and peace in believing, so that by the power of the Holy Spirit you may abound in hope."* Romans 15:13

Be blessed in your restored joy!

Peace

> *"Restore to me the joy of your salvation and grant me a willing spirit..."* Psalm 51:12

Today I'm Feeling:

_____

Today's Struggle:

_____

Small Victory Today:

_____

Where I Saw God Today:

_____

Prayer for Today:

_____

_____

_____

_____

_____

Reflect: When did I last feel true spiritual joy?

_____

_____

_____

_____

Chapter Reflection: What is keeping me from delighting in the Lord?

_____

_____

_____

_____

_____

Journal

_____

_____

_____

_____

_____

_____

_____

_____

_____

_____

_____

Doodle space:

Day 5 — Uphold Me with Thy Free Spirit

Every morning, I've gotten into this groove of chatting with God. I start by thanking Him and asking for blessings—not just for me, but for everyone around me. I dive into His Word with some devotions, and one of my favorites is Jesus Calling by Sarah Young. Today's message?

Trusting Him and being thankful will keep you going all day. Honestly, you can only do this with God's Holy Spirit by your side. So, why not invite Him in and see what unfolds?

At the end of his heartfelt prayer, David asked for God's "free" Spirit to help him navigate life. Now, "free" is an interesting take. When I dug into it, I found that the Hebrew word David used, "Navib," was translated by Luther as "princely," but other translations go with "generous" or "willing." Essentially, David was asking to break free from the confines of the Law. He wanted the freedom that comes from being cleansed of sin, ready to serve God and love others like He intended.

David longed for the Spirit to fill him up, driving away fear and worldly distractions while igniting a desire to live a life that pleases God.

> *"that we, being delivered from the hand of our enemies, might serve him without fear, in holiness and righteousness before him all our days."* Luke 1:74-75

We are truly living in freedom! God pours out His FREE Spirit, freeing us from sin and death. We embrace the resurrection of Christ as Easter people, breaking free from sin's chains. So, let's live with grateful, humble hearts like

David, fueled by God's Free Spirit. This Spirit empowers us to face each day without fear, living holy and righteous lives! Boy, that sounds EASY, right? (you can laugh; it was a joke)

Now, let's read Psalm51:10-12 again and meditate on David's cry. David was the poster child for sin, just like all of us, but he showed us how to genuinely repent. We know that if we come to Him with a contrite heart and ask for forgiveness, Christ's death and resurrection wipe the slate clean. We're doubly blessed when we invite His Holy and FREE Spirit to dwell in us, keeping us strong until we're united with Him for eternity.

Hey, my friends, you were called to be free! However, don't let that freedom turn into an excuse to indulge in whatever feels good; instead, let's *"serve each other with love and humility"*. (Galatians 5:13)

Stay blessed in your freedom!

Peace

"It is for freedom that Christ has set us free." Galatians 5:1

Today I'm Feeling:

_____

Today's Struggle:

_____

Small Victory Today:

_____

Where I Saw God Today:

_____

Prayer for Today:

_____

_____

_____

_____

_____

Reflect: What false burdens am I still trying to carry?

_____

_____

_____

_____

Chapter Reflection: How does God's Spirit invite me to live in freedom?

_____

_____

_____

_____

_____

Journal

_____

_____

_____

_____

_____

_____

_____

_____

Doodle space:

Day 6 — Peace Be with You

One of my favorite parts of the church service is sharing the peace. It's a time to show friendship, love, and forgiveness. I experienced something once which led me to have a whole new understanding and appreciation for this special gift.

> *"Jesus said to them again, 'Peace be with you. As the Father has sent me, even so I am sending you.'"* John 20:21

Years ago, I had a disagreement with a woman at my former church. One Sunday I had arrived late to church and, having an infant with me and needing a bit of room, the only spot I could find to sit was in the pew directly behind that woman. I began to get anxious; I knew that we would eventually have to face each other during the sharing of the peace.

Would she turn around? Would she reach her hand out to me? Should I offer my hand? Should I change seats? I prayed for guidance.

Before long, I heard Pastor call out, "The peace of the Lord be with you always," to which we faithfully responded, "And also with you."

Pastor continued: "We share God's peace." At that moment, the woman spun around, our eyes met with an apologetic look, we grasped each other's hands, smiled and, to each other, said, "Peace be with you."

Whatever happened in the past was buried. Whatever feelings we had were changed. Whatever friendship we previously had was reborn. We never spoke about our disagreement again but moved forward in Christian love and friendship. It was then when I began signing my emails and messages with "Peace".

> *"Finally, brothers, rejoice. Aim for restoration, comfort one another, agree with one another, live in peace; and the God of love and peace will be with you. Greet one another with a holy kiss."* 2 Corinthians 13:11-12

Sharing the peace is a time for restoration and encouraging one another!

If we reach out to one another in love and peace, imagine how blessed we will all be as Christian friends!

However, don't wait for that special time during service, share peace, love and friendship always and in all ways!

Peace be with you all!

Dear Lord,

We thank You for giving us a time to share peace and love with our brothers and sisters in Christ. Continue to send us Your peace and love, as we share Your blessings with others. In Jesus' name.

Amen

> *"Again Jesus said, 'Peace be with you! As the Father has sent me, I am sending you."* John 20:21

Today I'm Feeling:

_____

Today's Struggle:

_____

Small Victory Today:

_____

Where I Saw God Today:

_____

Prayer for Today:

_____

_____

_____

_____

_____

Reflect: Where do I need peace right now — internally or externally?

_____

_____

_____

_____

Chapter Reflection: How is God's peace different from the world's version?

_____

_____

_____

_____

Journal

_____

_____

_____

_____

_____

_____

_____

_____

Doodle space:

Day 7 — How Great Thou Art

Get your tissues, read this, read it again, then read it another ten times.

O Lord my God, When I in awesome wonder,
Consider all the worlds Thy Hands have made;
I see the stars, I hear the rolling thunder,
Thy power throughout the universe displayed.

When through the woods, and forest glades I wander,
And hear the birds sing sweetly in the trees.
When I look down, from lofty mountain grandeur
And see the brook, and feel the gentle breeze.

And when I think, that God, His Son not sparing;
Sent Him to die, I scarce can take it in;
That on the Cross, my burden gladly bearing,
He bled and died to take away my sin.

When Christ shall come, with shout of acclamation,
And take me home, what joy shall fill my heart.
Then I shall bow, in humble adoration,
And then proclaim: "My God, how great Thou art!"

Then sings my soul, My Savior God, to Thee
How great Thou art, how great Thou art
Then sings my soul, My Savior God, to Thee
How great Thou art, how great Thou art!

Crying yet? Not quite? Then do a web search for a video of Carrie Underwood's rendition. You're welcome.

Okay, buckle up buttercups. If you're not already a puddle of feelings after reading those words, just wait. Seriously, try to wrap your brain around a God so HUGE He flung stars into space like glitter (you know, functional glitter that makes galaxies – not available on Amazon, I checked).

And then this same God? He's noticing the little chickadees singing their hearts out in the backyard. It's enough to make you feel simultaneously microscopic and yet completely seen.

And don't even get me STARTED on the part about Him sending His own Son...like, come on. Talk about a love that'll knock you sideways.

You think your sacrifices are a big deal? Pssht. So yeah, grab those tissues. Carrie's gonna take it from here and just... unleash the waterworks. You've been warned.

> *"Great is the Lord and most worthy of praise; his greatness no one can fathom."* Psalm 145:3

Today I'm Feeling:

_____

Today's Struggle:

_____

Small Victory Today:

_____

Where I Saw God Today:

_____

Prayer for Today:

_____

_____

_____

_____

_____

Reflect: What has God done that deserves my loudest praise?

_____

_____

_____

_____

_____

Chapter Reflection: How does praising God's greatness strengthen my faith in what He will do next?

_____

_____

_____

_____

Journal

_____

_____

_____

_____

_____

_____

_____

_____

_____

Weekly Reflection

Where did I see God's faithfulness show up this week?

_____

_____

_____

_____

_____

What do I want to remember when things get tough again?

_____

_____

_____

_____

_____

Where have I come from — and where is God leading me next?

_____

_____

_____

_____

_____

Biggest Growth Moment:

_____

_____

_____

_____

_____

Biggest Struggle:

_____

_____

_____

_____

_____

Where I Saw God Working:

_____

_____

_____

_____

_____

Bible Verse that Moved Me:

_____

_____

_____

_____

_____

What I'm Carrying into Next Week:

_____

_____

_____

_____

_____

10 Ways to Surrender Throughout the Week

☐ 1. Start the day with prayer instead of phone scrolling

☐ 2. Hand over one worry in prayer

☐ 3. Take a break when overwhelmed and invite God into the chaos

☐ 4. Speak kindly when it's hard

☐ 5. Let go of needing to be right

☐ 6. Say 'no' when it's the healthier choice

☐ 7. Trust God's timing — not your own

☐ 8. Ask for help

☐ 9. Extend grace to yourself

☐ 10. Praise God in the middle of a mess

Gratitude List

1._____

_____

2._____

_____

3._____

_____

4._____

_____

5._____

Weekly Memory Verse Challenge

Write this week's memory verse below. Decorate it. Doodle it. Memorize it. Make it yours!

Memory Verse:

_____

_____

_____

_____

_____

Doodle space:

Week 7

Called, Not Comfortable— Purpose, Boldness & Kingdom Work

You weren't saved to sit still. Time to step up, speak out, and shine bright. You've been refined, healed, and equipped — now God's saying, "Let's go."

This week we get brave, bold, and a little bossy with the devil. You weren't built for the background — you were made to move mountains.

Guided Prayer to Start the Week

God, give me boldness to walk in my calling. Remind me that I don't need to feel qualified — I just need to be willing. Speak through me, move through me, and help me live like I know I was made for more.

Amen.

> *"For we are God's handiwork, created in Christ Jesus to do good works..."* Ephesians 2:10

Day 1 — Reasons and Seasons

Think about your first friend... do you remember how old you were? My first friend was my neighbor when we were very little. We grew up together; our parents still live next door to each other. She was my oldest and most dear friend; I could call her any time of night, any day, and she'd be there for me. She was the kind of friend with whom you can lose contact for a year but call each other and can pick up right where you left off.

Some friends come into our lives and are only there for a short while. They come, last a few years, and, though you didn't necessarily part on bad terms or from unpleasant circumstances, you just seem to drift apart. Some friends we make during childhood, some in adulthood. Some friends stick, others don't.

All the friends we have had teach us something about who we are and who we want to be. A true friend doesn't judge. A true friend is there when you need him/her. A true friend supports, edifies, encourages and comforts you. Sometimes a friend even needs to give you a reality check and challenge you.

However, there are those in our lives who we call "friends" who seem to hurt us. Are they true friends? Why does it hurt so badly? I know that, in my own familiar relationships, I have been hurtful. I don't mean to hurt them, I am sorry for it, but it's part of being a sinful human being.

I am forgiven because my family loves me. Why not forgive those friends who hurt us? After all, we love them, too, and consider them "family."

Yes, there are those by whom I have been hurt to the point where I do not wish to carry on as friends. Hardly a day goes by without my thinking of them in some capacity. I still love them; I still wish them well. It is also part of being a human being.

To all my friends, those who have come and gone, to those who I have hurt and those who have hurt me, in some capacity, you will be in my life forever. Thank you for helping to make me who I am today. I promise to be the best friend I can for you. You have supported me, built me up, encouraged me, comforted me, and even set me straight at times. I am forever indebted to you. I love you.

My first friend? She went to be with Jesus in 2013. I miss her every day. She was there for a season and a reason.

Dear God,

Thank You for the friends You've brought into my life. I know I've messed up sometimes and have not been nearly the kind of friend I should be. I've been selfish, distracted, or just not there. I'm sorry. Help me be the kind of friend who loves unconditionally, shows up, and stays. The kind of friend who will pick up the phone at any hour of the day or night. Heal any hurt I've caused, and keep my heart soft, kind, and loyal.

Finally, Lord, thank You for Jesus, the ultimate Friend. Please bless all my friends and keep them close to You.

Amen.

> *"There is a time for everything, and a season for every activity under the heavens."* Ecclesiastes 3:1

Today I'm Feeling:

_____

Today's Struggle:

_____

Small Victory Today:

_____

Where I Saw God Today:

_____

Prayer for Today:

_____

_____

_____

_____

_____

Reflect: What season of life am I in — and what is God asking of me right now?

_____

_____

_____

_____

_____

Chapter Reflection: How can I live with purpose even when things feel temporary or uncertain?

_____

_____

_____

_____

_____

_____

Journal

_____

_____

_____

_____

_____

_____

_____

_____

_____

_____

_____

Doodle space:

Day 2 — Faith, Hope and Love

> *"So now faith, hope, and love abide, these three; but the greatest of these is love."* 1 Corinthians 13:13

These three little words have been an amazing theme in my life for the last couple of years. Each word adding to who I am, what I want to do, and who I want to be, are like the necessary ingredients in the Kim recipe from the best chef in the world. In this case, God is the chef, I'm His "signature dish".

I began a Facebook page several years ago that was a great source of comfort for me during a difficult time. I posted inspirational, uplifting, encouraging, and supportive quotes that I hoped would help others as they did me. Sometimes friends will send me a quote to post, but I mainly just do a Google search for quotes that reflect my feelings for those moments.

> *"When I am afraid, I put my trust in you."* Psalm 56:3

> *"The Lord is near to the brokenhearted and saves the crushed in spirit."* Psalm 34:18

This book was created with a similar goal (because sometimes my own words just work better LOL kidding, move along). What words or phrases often run through your mind when you need to comfort someone? Do any hold special sentimental value or are they simply words of encouragement? Has anyone ever said something that gave you pause or gave you peace? (Um, yeah, how about God? The Bible IS His Word!)

I urge you to dig deep, get yourself a little notebook at the dollar store (Buck and a Quarter store now) and write down some emotions and meaningful words (hope, discouraged, love, faith, fear, etc.).

> *"Your word is a lamp to my feet and a light to my path."* Psalm 119:105

> *"Let the word of Christ dwell in you richly, teaching and admonishing one another in all wisdom, singing psalms and hymns and spiritual songs, with thankfulness in your hearts to God."* Colossians 3:16

Now you can start doing your homework. Get a snack, a cuppa coffee (maybe a glass of ____?) and get busy looking up Bible verses about each of the words you wrote. Write down everything you find. Try looking up just one of your words each day! Spend 10-15 minutes working in your notebook. Draw some doodles! Every so often, go back and read your previous entries.

Feel anything?

Better? Thought so.

Look at it like this: it's like making your own personal devotion book! Created by you, for you, but with all HIS WORDS! My prayer for you is that it's a constant source of inspiration, comfort, peace, and joy! There will be other times I tell you to get a notebook, so maybe treat yourself to a pretty one, a 5-subject, or one of those cool little binders that you can get different types of pages to insert. Oooh! Stickers! Go get some stickers!

"May the God of hope fill you with all joy and peace in believing, so that by the power of the Holy Spirit you may abounding hope." Romans 15:13

Again, I reflect:

"And now these three remain: faith, hope and love. But the greatest of these is love." 1 Corinthians 13:13

Today I'm Feeling:

_____

Today's Struggle:

_____

Small Victory Today:

_____

Where I Saw God Today:

_____

Prayer for Today:

_____

_____

_____

_____

_____

Reflect: Which of these three do I need to lean into most today, faith, hope, or love?

_____

_____

_____

_____

_____

Chapter Reflection: How do these three spiritual pillars shape how I show up in the world?

_____

_____

_____

_____

_____

Journal

_____

_____

_____

_____

_____

Doodle space:

Day 3 — Faith, Hope and Love, Part 2

I have a charm bracelet that I received as a young girl. It has your typical, silver charms: Christmas, birthday, a cute little bicycle with spinning wheels. Though one of the charms was always my favorite: "Faith, Hope and Charity," the cross, anchor and heart all on one link. I've always been drawn to these symbols (I even went to college in Rhode Island where the state symbol is the anchor and motto is "Hope"!)

Coincidence? You KNOW how I feel about coincidences.

I think that those icons are a part of who I am. My faith was instilled in me from day one. I was blessed with the presence of the Holy Spirit through my baptism when I was only a couple months old. Regularly attended Sunday School, church, served as an acolyte during my time as a confirmand. I have never wavered nor doubted my belief in God. Life has taken me on quite a journey, sometimes scary, sometimes confusing, sometimes fun, but always edifying: God's path for me always allowed my faith to grow.

Boy, do I still have so much to learn about faith!

The hope I have in my forever-life through Christ has allowed my faith to grow as I matured as a Missouri Synod Lutheran. Being privileged to serve in various capacities in the church, Council chair for several different committees, epistle reader, choir member (for decades!) and raising two children in the church have kept my focus clear that my God is a generous, loving and merciful god.

As time passed, I began to substitute the word "charity" for "love" as it appears in many Bible translations, though I will never abandon the word charity. Meaning "something given to a person in need" or "benevolent feeling, especially toward those in need or in disfavor", charity COMES FROM love. Charity IS love, the ultimate love, love from our Heavenly Father who knew we needed saving; we were in disfavor but are now given His grace and mercy!

This is our charge: to spread His love and to show love to others.

Gracious, loving God,

Thank you for these three amazing words to live by: faith, hope and love. I ask you to always be with me as I try to

Amen

> *"And hope does not put us to shame, because God's love has been poured out into our hearts..."* Romans 5:5

Today I'm Feeling:

_____

Today's Struggle:

_____

Small Victory Today:

_____

Where I Saw God Today:

_____

Prayer for Today:

_____

_____

_____

_____

_____

Reflect: How does hope empower me to keep going?

_____

_____

_____

_____

Chapter Reflection: What's something I can do today that expresses faith, hope, or love in action?

_____

_____

_____

_____

_____

Journal

_____

_____

_____

_____

_____

_____

_____

_____

_____

Doodle space:

Day 4 — Life... it's Past, Present, Future... Forever

People, places, things, events

Love, hate, trust, succeed, fail, cry, laugh

Every moment of everyday shapes who we are, what we feel, what we do in the future. We meet people and they are either gone in a flash or stay for a time (here for a season or here for a reason). However, we feel something with each one... we are changed.

Pets are like people we meet. We might pass a stranger walking a dog and stop to pet it. If the dog is friendly, we feel it... if the dog bites, we feel it (physically as well as emotionally!)

Sometimes we might have the privilege of owning a pet. That animal becomes a part of the family... a part of us... a part of who we are, what we feel, what we do in the future.

Such is the case when Pax came into my life. He was a part of me. He changed my life forever. I recall the day I had to let him go. He suddenly became very sick and I was forced to make a horribly difficult decision, one that changed not only Pax's life, but mine and that of everyone who had the honor of knowing him. I wasn't ready, but I had to do it. When that moment came, I looked into his eyes and whispered "I love you" over and over until he succumbed... somehow in those last moments I felt his love, too.

In a different chapter I speak about agape. I truly felt that unconditional love between me and Pax. I saw it also in my daughters and how they were with him. Pax truly loved Anabela, and she loved him. She was his "person".

We thank you, Pax, for loving so unconditionally, for being such a trusted friend. Though you only joined us for 9 years, a short time, you taught us more about love, responsibility, friendship and family than some do in their whole lives. You made us laugh, you made us cry, you taught us how to love HARD. You have changed our lives forever and we will always love you.

A loving and loyal relationship with a pet can be seen as a positive aspect of our lives, reflecting God's good creation and our role as responsible stewards. The joy, companionship, and unconditional love we experience with our pets can even give us a SMALL glimpse into the depth and steadfastness of God's love for us.

So, while God doesn't say, "Thou shalt have a black cocker spaniel named Sparky and love him dearly," the principles within Scripture certainly support the idea that the bond with a loving pet is a good and meaningful part of life within God's creation. God made 'em. End of story. He's got a soft spot for all His creatures, big and small, slobbery and furry (still don't understand mosquitos, but ok... just one question: how did they make it onto the Ark?).

God, in His boundless love and creativity, gave us dogs as faithful companions—loyal, joyful, and always ready to love us just as we are. Their devotion mirrors the kind of unconditional love He shows us every day. While the Bible doesn't mention dogs in the cozy, cuddly way we think of them today, it's clear that God delights in His creation and gives us good gifts to bring comfort and joy. Our furry friends are just one more way He whispers, "You are loved."

Pets make us happy, give us someone to talk to, who doesn't talk back, who won't judge our Netflix binges. We're supposed to be good caretakers – it's part of the gig He gave us in Genesis. That whole loyalty and love thing dogs give us? It's a cool little echo of the crazy, never-ending love God's got for us. So, yeah, loving your dog? Probably not a sin.

Now, if you'll excuse me, someone's demanding belly rubs and ear scritches.

> *"Jesus Christ is the same yesterday and today and forever."* Hebrews 13:8

Today I'm Feeling:

_____

Today's Struggle:

_____

Small Victory Today:

_____

Where I Saw God Today:

_____

Prayer for Today:

_____

_____

_____

_____

_____

Reflect: Where have I seen God's consistency in my life?

_____

_____

_____

_____

Chapter Reflection: How does knowing Jesus never changes give me confidence for the future?

_____

_____

_____

_____

Journal

_____

_____

_____

_____

_____

_____

_____

_____

_____

_____

_____

_____

Doodle space:

Day 5 — Divine Intervention

Have you ever missed a green light, only to watch another car speed through the intersection and get hit by someone running a red? And you can't help but wonder: Why wasn't that me?

Or maybe you've heard the stories—about people who worked at the World Trade Center but, for some mysterious reason, missed their train or called in sick on that tragic morning of September 11, 2001.

Coincidence? I don't believe in coincidences. I believe in a sovereign, omnipotent God.

For those of you who know me, none of this will come as a shock. I lean hard on my faith. I trust that God's hand is on every part of my life. Ok, ok... me being the control freak that I am does NOT live up to that claim. It's a daily struggle.

My writing may not always shine that through perfectly (and Lord knows I'm a work in progress), but I pray you'll keep reading anyway. I truly believe that "we know that for those who love God all things work together for good, for those who are called according to his purpose." (Romans 8:28).

Everything that happens—every delay, every unexpected moment—is part of His perfect plan. Yes, we have the freedom to choose, but He sends His Holy Spirit to guide us. Deep down, we often know the right path—we just need the courage to walk it.

C'mon, you know the words:

"... lead us not into temptation, but deliver us from evil" Matthew 6:13

Sometimes we don't realize how actively God is already answering that prayer for us.

Lately, I've been struggling with something heavy. A friend of mine - someone I love deeply—is not a follower of Christ. She calls herself a "white witch" and often speaks about practicing "white magic", whatever that is. Several times, she's asked to read my tarot cards. However, every time, my heart sinks. I know that Scripture is clear:

"Do not turn to mediums or necromancers; do not seek them out and so make yourselves unclean by them: I am the Lord your God." Leviticus 19:31

When I first learned about her practices last year, I ran to church the next morning with tears streaming down my face. I cried for her soul. I still do. I pray for her constantly. She even jokes that I'm always trying to convert her.

The truth? I've been too quiet. I regret not speaking the name of Jesus to her more boldly. Maybe her joking hints at a deeper guilt—an echo from her Catholic upbringing whispering that there's a better way, a true Light she's strayed from.

This is where divine intervention showed up yet again: One night, I went to her house for dinner. She talked all evening about wanting to read my cards. I kept praying silently, not knowing how to gracefully decline without hurting her feelings. Somehow, distraction after distraction kept popping up - until the evening ended and the cards stayed in the box. I didn't have to make an excuse. God simply steered the evening away. He knew I wasn't brave and bold enough to say what I SHOULD have.

> *"The Lord will fight for you; and you have only to be silent."* Exodus 14:14

Tomorrow evening, I'll go to church, and I'll probably cry again. I'll pray for strength to be His soldier—to stand firm in my faith without fear. I'll pray for the right words when the moment finally comes to lovingly share the truth with her. Most of all, I'll thank God for His incredible mercy—for yet another moment of divine intervention that spared me from compromising what I believe.

He is so faithful. Always.

> *"And who knows but that you have come to your royal position for such a time as this?"* Esther 4:14

Today I'm Feeling:

_____

Today's Struggle:

_____

Small Victory Today:

_____

Where I Saw God Today:

_____

Prayer for Today:

_____

_____

_____

_____

_____

Reflect: When have I experienced a "God moment" that shifted my path?

_____

_____

_____

_____

_____

Chapter Reflection: How is God placing me right where He needs me — even if it's uncomfortable?

_____

_____

_____

_____

_____

Journal

_____

_____

_____

_____

_____

_____

_____

_____

_____

Doodle space:

Day 6 — Favor

"What then shall we say to these things? If God is for us, who can be against us?" Romans 8:31

As I write this it's Sunday. It's one of my favorite days of the week. I'm up early enough to dawdle, enjoy a second cup of coffee, and have some devotion time before going to church and having 2 hours of faith-filled worship, praise and fellowship. It's a blessed day.

However, some Sundays don't always feel so blessed. My mind is not set right, and my heart isn't focused on my Savior. I let the earthly things (worry, drama, stress, anxiety, etc.) get in the way; in other words, I let Satan join me on my path instead of kicking him out and welcoming in the Holy Spirit.

This is EXACTLY when Satan loves to strike! When you choose to focus on God, you're at your best, you're feeling blessed, and love abounds. Beware! Satan is watching close by! He THRIVES on destroying those feelings because, if he does, he KNOWS you've pushed aside the Holy Spirit, and he walks right up to you. Like that proverbial "devil on your shoulder" whispering in your ear. He pulls your focus off of what's holy and pumps in doubt, fear, anger, sadness, even rage.

Today, I vow to try to keep myself focused on Godly things. I will do my best to keep my mind, heart and soul committed to my Heavenly Father. He routinely showers me with grace and mercy NO MATTER HOW MANY TIMES I WALK AWAY! I will CHOOSE to talk constantly to Him and ask Him to bless me.

One of my most favorite parts of Sunday worship is the Benediction. I absolutely feel His presence when those words are spoken. I am comforted by the reassurance that He is with me, protecting me, blessing me, smiling down on me. I have His Peace today and always. I just need to remember that when I'm feeling alone, defeated or stressed: He's got this!

> *"The Lord bless you and keep you; the Lord make his face to shine upon you and be gracious to you; the Lord lift up his countenance upon you and give you peace."* Numbers 6:24-26

Be blessed this day and always! Peace

> *"Surely, Lord, you bless the righteous; you surround them with your favor as with a shield."* Psalm 5:12

Today I'm Feeling:

_____

Today's Struggle:

_____

Small Victory Today:

_____

Where I Saw God Today:

_____

Prayer for Today:

_____

_____

_____

_____

_____

Reflect: Where do I need to trust that God's favor surrounds me even when I can't feel it?

_____

_____

_____

_____

_____

Chapter Reflection: How do I define "favor" — and how does God redefine it?

_____

_____

_____

_____

_____

Journal

_____

_____

_____

_____

_____

_____

_____

_____

_____

Doodle space:

Day 7 — The Best Gift

About a month after Christmas, I had an opportunity to enjoy the many gifts I received from family and friends, like a cordless drill (I dig tools), a cute little LED flashlight, a straw cleaning brush (don't laugh, I like neat things like that). However, I, of course, have tried my best to keep my focus on the best gift: grace and eternal life given through Christ.

Check this out. I recently read something I found interesting and profound:

> *"Over the past decade, Americans have purchased more than $1 trillion in gift cards. From 2005 to 2015 alone, unredeemed gift card balances totaled an astonishing $45.7 billion. That's a lot of unclaimed steak dinners, burrito bowls, and cups of coffee."* (December 29, 2024; oxygenfinancial.com)

Imagine! Over 45 billion dollars out there, purchased, but lost or forgotten... unredeemed.

Let that sink in a minute: billions of unredeemed gifts

Now compare that to the billions of people in the world and the billions "unredeemed" by Christ. There are approximately 8.2 billion people in the world today, yet only 2.38 billion are Christians. People without Christ are like gift cards unredeemed, someone paid for them, but they are lost or forgotten. Their cost was death on a cross, but what was bought is Glory.

We all as brothers and sisters in Christ have a calling to find the nearly 6 billion who haven't yet received their gifts! They aren't the ones sitting in the pews on Sundays, they are beyond the walls of the sanctuary, in the streets of your town, on a line at the grocery store, at work or school, in our own families.

Don't wait for Christmastime next year. You can give this amazing, precious, PREPAID gift all year round!

Peace, my friends.

> *"Thanks be to God for his indescribable gift!"* 2 Corinthians 9:15

Today I'm Feeling:

_____

Today's Struggle:

_____

Small Victory Today:

_____

Where I Saw God Today:

_____

Prayer for Today:

_____

_____

_____

_____

_____

Reflect: What is the best gift God has given me — and how
am I using it?

_____

_____

_____

_____

_____

Chapter Reflection: How does remembering the ultimate gift

of grace change how I live and love?

_____

_____

_____

_____

_____

_____

Journal

_____

_____

_____

_____

_____

_____

_____

_____

_____

Weekly Reflection

Where did I feel called to something bigger this week?

_____

_____

_____

_____

_____

What step of obedience did I take — even if it scared me?

_____

_____

_____

_____

_____

What gift or message do I need to keep using boldly?

_____

_____

_____

_____

_____

Biggest Growth Moment:

_____

_____

_____

_____

_____

Biggest Struggle:

_____

_____

_____

_____

_____

Where I Saw God Working:

_____

_____

_____

_____

_____

Bible Verse that Moved Me:

_____

_____

_____

_____

_____

What I'm Carrying into Next Week:

_____

_____

_____

_____

_____

10 Ways to Surrender Throughout the Week

☐ 1. Start the day with prayer instead of phone scrolling

☐ 2. Hand over one worry in prayer

☐ 3. Take a break when overwhelmed and invite God into the chaos

☐ 4. Speak kindly when it's hard

☐ 5. Let go of needing to be right

☐ 6. Say 'no' when it's the healthier choice

☐ 7. Trust God's timing — not your own

☐ 8. Ask for help

☐ 9. Extend grace to yourself

☐ 10. Praise God in the middle of a mess

Gratitude List

1._____

_____

2._____

_____

3._____

_____

4._____

_____

5._____

_____

Weekly Memory Verse Challenge

Write this week's memory verse below. Decorate it. Doodle it.
Memorize it. Make it yours!

Memory Verse:

_____

_____

_____

_____

_____

Doodle space:

Week 8

Cue the Confetti— Joy, Victory & Forward Momentum

You did the hard work. You let God wreck and restore you. Now it's time to dance in the grace, walk in the victory, and celebrate the glow-up of your faith. This week we honor the journey, praise the One who carried us, and look ahead with joy. Bring the glitter, grab the tissues, and get ready to walk out transformed.

Guided Prayer to Start the Week

God, thank You for being with me every step of this journey. Thank You for every breakthrough, every lesson, and every ounce of grace. Help me celebrate how far I've come and walk boldly into what's next.

Amen.

> *"He who began a good work in you will carry it on to completion..."* Philippians 1:6

Day 1 — Manic Moments & Lemon Meringue Grace

"Be still and know that I am God." Psalm 46:10

Here's the thing: I get ideas. A lot of them. Big ones. Creative ones. Emotional ones. I'll suddenly feel inspired—no, compelled—to start something new. Like journaling. Or organizing the entire house. Or blogging. Or baking a lemon meringue pie from scratch because, hey, zesting is basically therapy (second round of props to Aunt Peg!).

Recently, I started following a friend's blog – she's just "musing about life," as she puts it. And I thought: That's it! That's what I want to do.

I used to journal all the time. I should start blogging again. I have so much to say. I can be funny (See? That IS funny). I can be deep. I can be... wordy.

Here's what happens sometimes, though. I jump in headfirst with a rush of energy—writing, baking, organizing, dreaming—and then somewhere between post #2 and a sink full of dishes, I burn out. I've been here before. These "bursts" can feel like brilliance... or like chaos. And I often wonder: Is this real inspiration? Or just another manic episode in disguise?

I've come to realize that this rhythm—this rise and crash, this surge of energy followed by fog—isn't unfamiliar to God. He's not surprised by the whirlwind inside me. He's not frustrated by the fact that I sometimes start with fire and finish with ashes. He knows that's just who I am, and He meets me in the middle of the mania and the mess.

> *"Come to me, all who labor and are heavy laden, and I will give you rest."* Matthew 11:28

God doesn't need me to have it all together. He's not asking for polished writings or perfect pies or neatly filed paperwork. He wants my presence—my honest, scattered, real self. Even when my thoughts are racing and I can't sit still long enough to finish a devotion without checking my to-do list three times.

The truth is, whether I write for a day or a decade, whether I clean the whole house or just make lemon meringue pie and call it a win, God's love for me doesn't fluctuate with my productivity.

He is steady when I am spinning.

He is gentle when I am frayed.

He is present—even when I forget to be.

So, whether you're riding a wave of inspiration or just trying to stay afloat in the noise, remember: God is in both. He doesn't just show up when we're calm, focused, and consistent. He's with us in the burst, the burnout, and the beautifully messy in-between.

Father,

Thank You for loving me in every season—when I'm full of fire and when I'm running on empty. Help me to see Your hand in my inspiration and Your grace in my weariness. Teach me to be still, even when my mind is racing. And thank You for being the steady anchor in all my spinning.

Amen.

"The joy of the Lord is your strength." Nehemiah 8:10

Today I'm Feeling:

_____

Today's Struggle:

_____

Small Victory Today:

_____

Where I Saw God Today:

_____

Prayer for Today:

_____

_____

_____

_____

_____

Reflect: Where have I seen joy come from chaos?

_____

_____

_____

_____

_____

Chapter Reflection: How has God given me grace even when
I was a hot mess?

_____

_____

_____

_____

_____

Journal

_____

_____

_____

_____

_____

Doodle space:

Day 2 — The Love of a Dog

This morning, I woke up to Jazz enthusiastically licking my face. As soon as I rolled over, she flopped onto her back and waved her paws in the air like she was saying, "Your turn! Belly rubs, please!" (And yes, I know I said it would NEVER happen, but somehow, she's made herself at home in my bed!)

In one episode in this book, I spoke about Pax, our old dog who left us in November 2011. While no one could ever take his place, Jazz has bravely stepped in to fill that special spot in my heart reserved for a dog's love.

Pax was a lean, mean 120 lbs., while Jazz barely tips the scales at 15. But honestly, the love they give? It's colossal! Had a rough day? Just head home to your dog! They have a sixth sense for when you're feeling down or under the weather. Dogs are the ultimate combination of gentle, goofy, smart, and always ready for a good walk, a game of fetch, tug-of war, or just a cozy snuggle accompanied by a solid ear rub.

Pax and Jazz might be worlds apart in size and style, but Jazz somehow knows exactly what I need, just like Pax did.

I get that some folks are cat people – I once had a cat who was my buddy for nearly 17 years. But let's be real: in my opinion, no cat can give you the kind of love a dog does! Affection, loyalty, devotion, laughter, and that unshakeable support—it's a one-of-a-kind package! I know not everyone is a "dog person," but honestly, who wouldn't want to experience the incredible love of a dog at least once in their life? This reminds me of Proverbs 17:17:

"A friend loves at all times..."

While dogs aren't human friends or brothers in the traditional sense, the unwavering love and support they offer often mirror this kind of companionship. They are a constant source of comfort in the ups and downs of life.

Oh, my beloved Pax, at the beach on Fire Island or upstate by the river—the only lab I knew who absolutely hated the water! Yet, there he was, lugging 5 lb. rocks to help us build a dam or playfully patting a sand crab. Let's not even talk about the fireworks; he'd bolt to the camper like it was a bomb shelter. The moment you backed out of the driveway, he'd be lounging on the couch, and by the time you returned, the couch would still be warm from his "hard work."

Then there's my sweet little Jazz—sometimes playful, always sleepy, and often sassy! She's got brains, humor, and a heart full of love. *Jazzy, I really wish you could've met Pax; you two would've been the best of buds!*

Fast-forward to the summer of 2019. My girls started a campaign to get me to get another dog. *"PLEASE can we get another dog?"* must have been asked a minimum of a dozen times every day from June to August.

Then the question changed a little. It morphed into *"PLEASE can we get a dog - and if we get a dog, can it be a BIG dog? If we get a big dog can we name him 'Buddy'?"*

Oh, boy. The girls are getting really serious about this. I've never had two dogs at the same time before; could I handle it? Wait! What the h***?! Am I ACTUALLY considering this?

I'm allergic to dog and cat fur (dander?) so, Jazz has been perfect for me: never sheds and I can stick my nose deep into her soft hair (not fur) and breathe in deeply with no effect. There are no furballs tumbling throughout the house, no dog smell. Jazz gets groomed, so, as my girls say, she smells like "blueberries and diapers". Big dogs smell (except for my sweet Paxie, he was an angel... I actually just forget if he did or not).

One night, August 22, 2019 (you'll soon know why I remember the exact date), Eric and I are doing our typical summer evening "thing": chilling in the living room with a Mets game on. Gary, Keith, and Ron announcing is like the calmest, happiest tune playing softly as we scroll social media that rivals our kids' screen time.

"Hey, hun?" Eric asked sweetly.

"Um hm," I answered, keeping my nose in my Instagram.

"Do you wanna meet Buddy?" he asked softly as he slowly turned his tablet around to show me THE MOST BEAUTIFUL BOY IN THE WHOLE WIDE WORLD: Buddy - currently residing at Brookhaven Animal Shelter, a mere 5-minute drive from me.

Dammit. I just got another dog, didn't I?

He's just SO HANDSOME! I was in love already.

(God moment!)

The next day being Friday, a summer Friday, I was packed and ready to head down to the Jersey Shore as we do every weekend. Bela slept at her friend's house the night prior and I told her I'd be picking her up at 10am. She wasn't happy about having to get up early but begrudgingly agreed so we could go home and pack so we could get on the road by 12pm at the latest. She hopped in the car and was clearly still half asleep.

Handing her my car hairbrush (you have car lip balm, let me have my car hairbrush), I asked, "Can you please just brush your hair and make yourself look a little presentable? We have to stop somewhere first."

"No, Mom! Come on! WHY?! I just wanna go home and pack so we can go to Jersey!" I pulled up on my phone the shelter website, scrolled to the photo of my sweet, future, furry son, and showed her my screen. "So, we can go meet him: Buddy."

"NO WAY!!" she screamed as she suddenly woke up like she just downed 2 energy drinks. We arrived at the shelter, entered the lobby and went to the office window. I smiled and said, "Good morning! We'd like to meet Buddy."

Squeals from the workers inside. "AW! THEY'RE HERE FOR BUDDY! WE LOVE BUDDY!" and we were soon led to a room filled with mismatched sectional couches.

> *"Then our mouth was filled with laughter, and our tongue with shouts of joy; then they said among the nations, 'The Lord has done great things for them.' The Lord has done great things for us; we are glad."*
> Psalm 126:2-3

A large (read: tall and strong) young man appeared at the door to the room and seemed to be slightly struggling as he opened the door. In entered the man with Buddy on a leash, pulling the man's arm nearly out of its socket. The door closed behind them and Buddy was released from his tether.

Remember "Ricochet Rabbit"? As in "Bing bing BING! Ricocheeeettt Rabbit!" (If you don't, you're probably young... so, do a web search) Anyway, yeah, that instantly came to mind as Buddy bounced from sectional to sectional; flopping all around, he was the happiest boy! I loved him already.

"Hey, babe. It's me." I said as Eric answered his office phone. "Can you take your lunch early?"

"Um, yeah... I can take lunch anytime I want. Why?" he cautiously asked.

"So, you can come meet Buddy. The shelter needs to meet everyone in the home before I get approved to adopt him." I can just imagine the laughter bursting throughout his office and in his car as he drove to the shelter. He knows me so well, though, so he probably wasn't surprised.

We called Sara and Ian and they brought Jazz because the trainer needed to introduce the two dogs to evaluate their behavior together.

Eric arrived and approached the very clearly UNTRAINED Buddy who instantly rolled onto his back giving Eric his belly. Belly rubs... soon to be a daily treat for Bud. Eric was smitten. Ok, ok... I was, too. God gave me a "son".

Bring the two dogs toward each other now," the trainer said. Jazz and Buddy walked slowly and casually near each other, gave each other's bum a solid sniff (if they were human they would have then given each other a "Sup" nod), and walked apart to continue their multiple-dog-scent-everywhere quest.

"That's EXACTLY what we want to see," the trainer said. Let the paperwork commence.

Sara and Ian went to Shirley Feed to purchase a (very large) crate, bowls, food, collar, leash, and toys. I sat with the young man who brought me Buddy, and we went over the application and all the vital information I needed.

Normal adoption fees are around $500, but not for Buddy. I only had to pay $14! That covered the cost of changing his license to his "owner" (mom) being in my name. He was chipped, neutered, given all his shots, and heartworm, flea/tick meds administered. Apparently, a few weeks prior, a woman adopted him but brought him back that very same day saying he was "wild", "uncontrollable", and "bared his teeth" at her husband. She forfeited her now "donation" and Buddy went back to his pen at the shelter. She was not his mommy, I'M his mommy. God knew funds were a bit tight, so He had that lady take care of the fees! LOL (another God moment!)

For the record, that boy would NEVER bare his teeth or be aggressive with ANYONE. It's almost to a fault, because if we ever got robbed, he'd bring the robber his ball to play fetch.

Needless to say I did NOT go to the Jersey Shore that weekend. I stayed home with my boy (my son), still on a leash for a day and a half. He slept soundly and quietly in his crate, did his potty time outside like the good boy that he is. He is smart, SO funny, dopey, lovey, and hyper. Well, hyper not so much now as he's 7 years old and there's a new pup in our house (yes, another dog... I'll get to that eventually... that one needs her own chapter). He loves his stuffed animals (particularly his dinos), his ball, his Poppa (my dad), and most of all, his momma. He is my shadow, my bubbie, my sweet baby boy, and I love him with my whole heart.

Two words to wrap up the whole point of this chapter: God provides.

Seriously. You think it's just a coincidence (stop with the coincidences already... no such thing) that these furry, little weirdos wiggle their way into our lives and somehow glue our broken pieces back together? Nope. That's definitely not random.

God provides the love of a dog! It's like He looked down and said, "Hmm, they need a slobbery alarm clock and a ton of unconditional, albeit slightly drooly affection."

Then BAM! Instant, tail-wagging, lap-dogging therapy. It might seem simple, but honestly, isn't that just like God? Taking the everyday, seemingly insignificant to some, and using it to show us a love that's bigger than any tumble-fur in the living room. It's a furry, four-legged testament to HIS CONSTANT CARE.

"We love because he first loved us." 1 John 4:19

Today I'm Feeling:

_____

Today's Struggle:

_____

Small Victory Today:

_____

Where I Saw God Today:

_____

Prayer for Today:

_____

_____

_____

_____

_____

Reflect: Where did I experience unconditional love recently?

_____

_____

_____

_____

_____

Chapter Reflection: How does God's love for me show up in unexpected places?

_____

_____

Journal

_____

_____

_____

_____

_____

_____

_____

_____

_____

Doodle space:

Day 3 — The War

"But he knows the way that I take; when he has tried me, I shall come out as gold. My foot has held fast to his steps; I have kept his way and have not turned aside." Job 23:10-11

There's a war going on, and I'm involved; the battlefield is my mind and spirit. God and Satan are in a constant battle over my faith. Satan wants me as his own; he tests me, tempts me, and loves to put obstacles in my path, making me stumble and causing me to question my journey and my faith.

I make a daily effort to be a good person, although I can be nasty, overly sensitive, and very often, self-centered. As I reflect on this, I recognize my flaws. I am made up of SO many wrongs; I could never count them. I fear they cancel out the good I try to be. I worry my faith and spirit aren't strong enough to withstand what Satan throws at me, the tests God permits (I'm no Job). I forget who I'm dealing with.

Recently, I found myself dwelling on the things I "hate." Before long, I was sad, angry, overly critical, spiteful, and jealous—all traits that Satan loves about me; everything God does NOT want me to be.

- I hate when the bad guy wins.
- I hate when the good guy loses.
- I hate when the jock gets the cheerleader.
- I hate when those people WITH win things over others WITHOUT.

- I hate when someone steals the parking spot or chair I was waiting for.
- I hate when the weather ruins my plans.
- I hate passive-aggressive behavior.

I know, you're saying, "Pretty stupid cr@p, Kim. Get over yourself." I get that. I do. I have to get over it; and I will... eventually. However, when that "stupid cr@p" is happening, I'm pretty annoyed...and rather less-than- Christian to say the least.

Hence, the theme of this book. I am forever seeking a way I can be a good Christian AND be my normally sassy self. Can there really be balance? Do I have to become Pollyanna in order to be a good Christian woman? Or can I be a little María from the Sound of Music mixed with some Sister Mary Clarence? I am of the belief that God has an awesome sense of humor, so, why not?

So, I'm relearning how to react to daily occurrences such as the ones I mentioned above. Injustices, if you will. Things that pi$$ me off. Part of my relearning process is being able to recognize that I'm reacting, part of it is realizing it's just "stupid cr@p". When I stop and think about it all, the whole process, I remind myself that the good comes from God, and the bad is from Satan. Satan wants me to fail. He wants me to yell and scream and tantrum. He would LOVE if I became more like him.

So, I pray.

I su©k at praying, though.

I pray that I have the strength to see this for what it is and to get through it with love, grace and humility. Only God can help me get there. It's all part of the journey.

> *"Finally, brothers, whatever is true, whatever is honorable, whatever is just, whatever is pure, whatever is lovely, whatever is commendable, if there is any excellence, if there is anything worthy of praise, think about these things."* Philippians 4:8

I've been reading Job in my new study Bible. He had it all, then lost it all. God and Satan were at war over him too. Job had his moments, but throughout all the trials, his faith remained steadfast. Why do I let trivial matters affect me? Why do I allow Satan to prey on my weaknesses? I must remember that God's trials for me are meant to strengthen me, not to punish me. Yes, I'm a sinner, but He will always provide a way out.

> *"... even to your old age I am he, and to gray hairs I will carry you. I have made, and I will bear; I will carry and will save."* (Isaiah 46:4)

Heavenly Father, grant me the strength to see trials for what they are and help me navigate them with love, grace, humility, and faith. Guide me to recognize Your blessings amidst the challenges. I praise You for Your unwavering support and guidance. Help me to remain steadfast in my faith and to reflect Your love in all that I do.

Amen.

"In all these things we are more than conquerors through him who loved us." Romans 8:37

Today I'm Feeling:

_____

Today's Struggle:

_____

Small Victory Today:

_____

Where I Saw God Today:

_____

Prayer for Today:

_____

_____

_____

_____

Reflect: What battle have I won through God's help?

_____

_____

_____

_____

Chapter Reflection: How has God shown me victory even in weakness?

_____

_____

_____

_____

_____

Journal

_____

_____

_____

_____

_____

Doodle space:

Day 4 — A Message of Hope

From the song "When I Get Where I'm Going" by Brad Paisley and Dolly Parton:

> *"Yeah, when I get where I'm going, there'll be only happy tears. I will shed the sins and struggles I have carried all these years. And I'll leave my heart wide open; I will love and have no fear. Yeah, when I get where I'm going, don't cry for me down here."*

Jesus must have felt this way, though having carried our sins and struggles, as He walked toward His death. He knew that He had to fulfill what was prophesied; He was born to die, so that we may have eternal life. He did so willingly... "God willingly", so to speak.

As we meditate on Jesus, His life, His death, we must also remember this message of hope: *"But when I get where I'm going, and I see my Maker's face, I'll stand forever in the light of His amazing grace."*

Jesus knew why He had to die. Though the disciples and followers believed in Him and His promised resurrection, living it, as it happened, must have been heartbreaking, confusing and a test of their faith. How horrible they must have felt when Jesus breathed His last... hanging, tortured, bleeding on a cross as people mocked and scorned Him.

Didn't Christ's followers remember His promise of a "comeback"? Didn't they believe He would conquer death and return in 3 days? I can't wrap my brain around how He must have felt to know that his very best friends, his disciples and students, the ones who boasted about how much they love Him, had questioned their faith in Him (ahem, Thomas).

Thankfully, we don't have to witness Christ's torture and death firsthand, but we can certainly take that walk with Him through meditation, reading the Bible and devotions, and prayer. What we must always hold onto is the message of hope that He brings: through His death and resurrection, we are SAVED! I will see my Maker's face, and I will stand forever in the light of His amazing grace!

Lord God,

We thank You for sending Your Son to teach us Your message of hope; hope of a life eternally with You. Please send Your Holy Spirit to guide us as we ponder the wonder of Christ's resurrection and Your amazing grace. Until we get where we're going, we continue to praise you and worship you... Through Jesus Christ our Lord, Amen

> *"...remembering before our God and Father your work of faith and labor of love and steadfastness of hope in our Lord Jesus Christ."* 1 Thessalonians 1:3

> *"...because of the hope laid up for you in heaven. Of this you have heard before in the word of the truth, the gospel"* Colossians 1:5

> *"May the God of hope fill you with all joy and peace as you trust in him..."* Romans 15:13

Today I'm Feeling:

_____

Today's Struggle:

_____

Small Victory Today:

_____

Where I Saw God Today:

_____

Prayer for Today:

_____

_____

_____

_____

_____

Reflect: Where have I found hope that I didn't expect?

_____

_____

_____

_____

_____

Chapter Reflection: What hope am I holding onto for the future?

_____

_____

_____

_____

Journal

_____

_____

_____

_____

_____

_____

_____

Doodle space:

Day 5 — God Moments and A Burning Bush

In speaking with my husband last week, I was questioning my call in life, my purpose, my role, etc. My husband, being my spiritual slap-upside-the-head, simply said, "Pray. Ask God for a burning bush. Tell Him to be obvious." I did as he suggested.

Follow me on a little journey if you will...

1980-something: I sat my teenage-self in my bedroom, probably in a hormonal heap, and grabbed my Bible. I said to God, "I'm going to open this to a random page. I know it is what I'm supposed to read at this moment. Ok, here goes (and I opened it in the New Testament because we are "Easter People") He led me to 1 John 2, I read it, stuck my bookmark in it, and hoped that one day I would "get it".

> *"My little children, I am writing these things to you so that you may not sin. But if anyone does sin, we have an advocate with the Father, Jesus Christ the righteous. He is the propitiation for our sins, and not for ours only but also for the sins of the whole world. And by this we know that we have come to know him, if we keep his commandments. Whoever says "I know him" but does not keep his commandments is a liar, and the truth is not in him, but whoever keeps his word, in him truly the love of God is perfected. By this we may know that we are in him: whoever says he abides in him ought to walk in the same way in which he walked. Beloved, I am writing you no new commandment, but an old commandment that you*

had from the beginning. The old commandment is the word that you have heard. At the same time, it is a new commandment that I am writing to you, which is true in him and in you, because the darkness is passing away and the true light is already shining. Whoever says he is in the light and hates his brother is still in darkness. Whoever loves his brother abides in the light, and in him there is no cause for stumbling. But whoever hates his brother is in the darkness and walks in the darkness, and does not know where he is going, because the darkness has blinded his eyes." 1 John 2:1-11

1988: I learned that my college friend loves the song "Baby, I Love Your Way" (I know, it seems detached... hang in there)

2011: I wrote my first blog (felt it to be cathartic and exhilarating... until I got writer's block)

2014: I wrote my first devotion (again cathartic and exhilarating... until I got massive writer's block)

2016: I reconnected with that old college friend on Facebook after almost 30 years... she's not big into Facebook, though

2017: I began another blog... until I got writer's block... again

2018: I prayed that God would blatantly tell me what He wants me to do

2019: I wrote about 1 Peter4:16 and shared on social media; over the course of the day and evening I received several comments from friends thanking me for posting verses and devotions, how they look forward to them, etc.

6:30am: WBAB played "Baby, I love your Way" … I remembered my old college friend loved that song and thought, "I wonder how she's doing?"

9:28am: I received a private message from that dear, old friend (first words since reconnecting a year and a half prior) in which she thanked me for my (faith) posts every day and asked for prayers for her husband who is battling cancer… she is scared and clearly searching for strength through her faith

9:30am: I shared the story with a friend (a brother in Christ) at work about my 1 Peter 4:16 post and the incredible message I had just received… he shared with me a poem that was about being the light and how that is scarier to us than shrinking into darkness so as to make others more comfortable… he said it's by Marianne Williamson and I vowed to look it up

11am: I stopped in to chat with another friend and, in wanting to show her a picture of my daughter on Facebook, and, upon opening the app, I found that my friend, Cathy (photographer extraordinaire), had posted THAT VERY SAME QUOTE by Marianne Williamson

12pm: I realized God was practically shaking me by my shoulders yelling at me, "You wanted a burning bush! Here's your burning bush! Now go write! Go share! Don't ever be ashamed of being the light!"

I got my burning bush.

Peace to you all

> *"God called to him from within the bush, 'Moses! Moses!' And Moses said, 'Here I am.'"* Exodus 3:4

Today I'm Feeling:

_____

Today's Struggle:

_____

Small Victory Today:

_____

Where I Saw God Today:

_____

Prayer for Today:

_____

_____

_____

_____

_____

Reflect: What moment has felt like God calling my name?

_____

_____

_____

_____

_____

Chapter Reflection: How am I responding when God calls me to something bigger?

_____

_____

_____

_____

Journal

_____

_____

_____

_____

_____

_____

_____

_____

Doodle space:

Day 6 — Create in Me...

"Create in me a clean heart, O God, and renew a right spirit within me. Cast me not away from your presence, and take not your Holy Spirit from me. Restore to me the joy of your salvation, and uphold me with a willing spirit." Psalm 51:10–12

Let me just say—this is one of my favorite passages in the entire Bible. Hands down. If you grew up on the old-school Lutheran liturgy like I did, you probably heard this one sung in your head like the Offertory. (Don't lie, you're humming it right now.)

It's rich. It's raw. It's real. It's forever on the playlist of your life.

This psalm is David's full-on spiritual meltdown after realizing how deep he was in sin. We're not talking about forgetting to tithe or muttering under your breath in traffic. We're talking adultery, lies, manipulation, and murder. David didn't dip his toe into sin—he cannonballed in.

And yet, what does he do?

He cries out: *"Create in me a clean heart."*

Here's the thing—David didn't ask for a heart polish. He didn't ask for a tune-up. He asked God to create a clean heart. The original Hebrew word for "create" here—bara—is the kind of creation only God can do. It's not "redecorate your heart with a Pinterest Bible verse." It's "burn it down and start from scratch." A total spiritual renovation. And really, that's what I need too.

Let's be honest: I have a pile of sins. I sin daily, hourly... sometimes by accident, sometimes with full awareness and just enough attitude to justify it to myself. (I said what I said. Sorry, not sorry... okay, a little ? no, A LOT sorry.)

Here's the hard truth: God doesn't line our sins up and grade them on a curve. A lie, a tantrum, a full-blown David-style disaster—they all fall short of His glory. Sin is sin. That's why we don't get a gold star for "trying really hard." That's why we need Jesus.

In the Lutheran Church, we hold fast to the Luther's teachings of the Bible that it's not *our* doing that saves us—it's all Christ.

Sola Gratia (by grace alone)

Sola Fide (through faith alone)

Solus Christus (in Christ alone)

(if you didn't already know, there are 2 other "Solas", by the way; I love the Solas).

Through the gift of Baptism, the Word, and the Sacraments, God does what we can't: He creates in us new hearts and renews our spirits every single day.

That "joy of Your salvation" David talks about? I want that. I need that. Because honestly, life can wear me down and steal that joy in a heartbeat.

When I remember that Jesus is my joy—that He's already won, already cleansed, already covered me in grace—that's when I can breathe again.

So, today, I'm praying:

Lord, create in me what only You can. Make me new. Not just cleaner - new. Keep me close to You, don't let me wander too far, and restore that joy that only Your salvation can bring.

Amen

Today I'm Feeling:

_____

Today's Struggle:

_____

Small Victory Today:

_____

Where I Saw God Today:

_____

Prayer for Today:

_____

_____

_____

_____

_____

_____

_____

Reflect: What new thing is God doing in my heart?

_____

_____

_____

_____

_____

Chapter Reflection: Where am I seeing real transformation begin?

_____

_____

_____

_____

_____

Journal

_____

_____

_____

_____

_____

_____

_____

_____

_____

_____

_____

_____

_____

_____

Doodle space:

Day 7 — Final Encouragement & Blessing (Will This Book Thing Work Out?)

Spoiler alert: If you're reading this final chapter, the answer is already "yes." Not because I crafted some literary masterpiece or solved all of life's problems in these pages, but because God, in His infinite wisdom (and boundless patience with my sass), works ALL things together for good — even unfinished books by Type-A Christian moms with a love of label makers and labradors.

Being a life-long Lutheran Church—Missouri Synod (LCMS) Lutheran has taught me a few things that kept me from giving up somewhere between "Life as a Type-A" and "10 Things I Can't Live Without." Most importantly, that it's not about *me*. It's about Christ.

Always has been.

Always will be.

I mentioned it earlier, but remember what God's Word promises in Romans 8:28,

"And we know that for those who love God all things work together for good, for those who are called according to his purpose."

Notice it doesn't say "only perfectly organized, beautifully footnoted, best-selling things." Just "all things." Even former blog posts that morphed into half devotionals, half dog stories, half "please-get-it together" pep talks. (Yes, I know that's three halves. Math isn't my gift. Grace is.)

Throughout this book, we've laughed at my grocery store meltdowns, cried with the memories of beloved pets, groaned at teenage dramas, and marveled at God's undeniable fingerprints on the mundane moments of life. That's because we live in the "now and not yet" tension – a classic LCMS theme. We are saved, and yet we struggle.

We are saints, and yet we are sinners. (In my case, a rather snarky one.) My homeboy, Martin Luther, got it right: *"We are beggars. This is true."*

Every chapter of our lives, whether it's titled "God Moments" or "mean," reflects how desperately we need Jesus to redeem the mess. Thankfully He does — by grace alone, through faith alone, in Christ alone!

So, will this book thing work out? Well, if by "work out" we mean "convince the New York Times to call me," probably not. But if we mean "proclaim Christ crucified and risen" and "encourage someone to talk to God like a friend again," then yes. A thousand times yes.

Luther once said, *"Even if I knew that tomorrow the world would go to pieces, I would still plant my apple tree today."* I suppose writing this book was my apple tree. Small, humble, quirky, maybe a little misshapen (ok, a LOT misshapen) — but planted firmly in the hope of the resurrection. Because no matter how cracked the pottery, the Potter's hands never slip. (Good one, huh? I stole it... no credit for that one)

My prayer is simple: May you laugh a little more, pray a little more, forgive a little quicker, and cling to Christ with all your glorious, flawed, beloved heart.

Thanks for walking this crooked, grace-soaked road with me.

Your Friendly, Sassy, Flawed, Sister in Faith,

Kim

"And I am sure of this, that he who began a good work in you will bring it to completion at the day of Jesus Christ." Philippians 1:6

(P.S. If we ever meet in person, you bring the duct tape and chocolate. I'll bring bungee cords, my P-Touch, and a Bible. It'll work out. Trust me.)

Today I'm Feeling:

_____

Today's Struggle:

_____

Small Victory Today:

_____

Where I Saw God Today:

_____

Prayer for Today:

_____

_____

_____

_____

_____

Reflect: What is God still doing in me that's just beginning?

_____

_____

_____

_____

_____

Chapter Reflection: What encouragement do I want to carry forward from this journey?

_____

_____

_____

_____

Journal

_____

_____

_____

_____

_____

_____

_____

_____

_____

Weekly Reflection

What transformation have I seen in myself over these 8 weeks?

_____

_____

_____

_____

_____

What promise of God am I holding onto now?

_____

_____

_____

_____

_____

_____

What's next — and how can I walk boldly into it with God?

_____

_____

_____

_____

_____

_____

Biggest Growth Moment:

_____

_____

_____

_____

_____

Biggest Struggle:

_____

_____

_____

_____

_____

_____

Where I Saw God Working:

_____

_____

_____

_____

_____

Bible Verse that Moved Me:

_____

_____

_____

_____

_____

What I'm Carrying into Next Week:

_____

_____

_____

_____

_____

_____

10 Ways to Surrender Throughout the Week

☐ 1. Start the day with prayer instead of phone scrolling

☐ 2. Hand over one worry in prayer

☐ 3. Take a break when overwhelmed and invite God into the chaos

☐ 4. Speak kindly when it's hard

☐ 5. Let go of needing to be right

☐ 6. Say 'no' when it's the healthier choice

☐ 7. Trust God's timing — not your own

☐ 8. Ask for help

☐ 9. Extend grace to yourself

☐ 10. Praise God in the middle of a mess

Gratitude List

1._____

_____

2._____

_____

3._____

_____

4._____

_____

5._____

_____

Weekly Memory Verse Challenge

Write this week's memory verse below. Decorate it. Doodle it. Memorize it. Make it yours!

Memory Verse:

_____

_____

_____

_____

_____

_____

Doodle space (a big one, so go for it!):

12 Bonus Essays

As promised! I did not add journal space for the following essays. However, please feel free to visit *www.favordeipress.com* to download and print free, blank journal/devotional pages. Or get that cool notebook I mentioned.

The Good in Everyone

Smiles, jokes, laughter, uplifting quotes, songs, and passages... imagine life without them. Are you even able to?

So, I consider myself to be a rather upbeat, positive person. I definitely have "laugh lines" around my eyes; I smile and laugh a lot. I trust easily, I commit easily, and I love easily. I am honest and forthcoming.

Likewise, I think everyone is the same and I truly believe there is good in everyone. This makes me vulnerable by exposing my biggest weaknesses. The challenge is to continue doing good and treating others the way we were instructed:

> *"And as you wish that others would do to you, do so to them."* Luke 6:31

> *"A new commandment I give to you, that you love one another: just as I have loved you, you also are to love one another. By this all people will know that you are my disciples, if you have love for one another."* John 13:34-35

> *"Be kind to one another, tenderhearted, forgiving one another, as God in Christ forgave you."* Ephesians 4:32

As I travel through life day by day, various events jar my faith, my confidence, my hope. I try so hard to tap into my inner optimist; I always try to be happy, seeking the positive. It's SO DIFFICULT, though! Our world is so broken, and Satan is everywhere. He doesn't WANT us to be happy, positive, loving, or trusting in God. He thrives on our anxiety, grief, negativity, and anger. Satan LOVES to see us become vulnerable and hurting and he'll do everything he can to make sure you don't reach out to God for His comfort and guidance. He'll slither into our brains just when we think everything is cool, life is good... he's counting on us to not give all thanks and praise to God, but to "forget" where we get all our blessings.

However, that vulnerability I mentioned exists at times and can be unnerving. I find myself suppressing the hurt, the pain, the anger, the grief, the anxiety. I don't show it, but I feel it. Until I break like a piece of fine china dropped from a rooftop to the pavement. I shatter into a million pieces and remain as such until I scoop myself up and put myself back together.

How long will I stay that way? Depends on a lot of factors: who is present or available for me to vent to, where I am (work, not cool; church, cool), and if I'm being dead honest, if I've consumed any adult beverages that would distort my conception of reality. Friends and family may try to help if they are blessed enough to be around, but in the end, I need to focus on my own happiness. That's where God comes in, because, inevitably, I forget to confer with Him first before losing it, but He is the only one who is going to get me through it.

> *"Rejoice in hope, be patient in tribulation, be constant in prayer."* Romans 12:12

Quite a few years ago I had the privilege of teaching Character Education. I admit I was nervous and worried the first year I was assigned to teach it, but soon I grew to not only love the kids in the class, but the content of the curriculum as well. Together we spoke about love, honesty, trust, generosity, and my favorite: integrity. (All the kids knew that "integrity" is my favorite.) I try to bring a positive disposition with me every day, even if I don't particularly feel it. I know that, in sharing with the kids, they will scoop me up like that shattered piece of china and I will inevitably (in the span of 42 minutes) feel whole again.

Sometimes, in discussion, a student will mention a negative character trait. To me it's like nails on a chalkboard; I try my hardest to redirect being positive. I want my students to be comfortable to be themselves, but to also want to BE good, to DO good all on their own, and to believe there IS indeed good in every person. Years later I think about those kids and pray they took a little something (positive) with them from that class.

My fear of teaching that class was unnecessary, unfounded, unreasonable. It's a perfect example of finding the blessing in everything.

> *"Rejoice in the Lord always; again, I will say, Rejoice."* Philippians 4:4

We may not show or see it every day in everything we do, but one of my goals is to share a little goodness and to teach others to do so as well. In general, I am at peace (most of the time). It's my default and I'll always land there with the help of God.

> *"May the God of hope fill you with all joy and peace in believing, so that by the power of the Holy Spirit you may abound in hope."* Romans 15:13"

Why I Do What I Do Today

I had the pleasure of getting together with a former student. She was probably one of the toughest nuts to crack throughout my nearly 30+ years of teaching, but she and I became very close when she was in my class. I still remember the first day I met her: I was calling the students' names out on the first day of school, trying to memorize their faces as well. Her last name was Portuguese, and I asked her, "Fala portugues?"

She, amidst her poor attitude and behavior, answered, "Sim, falo." At that moment we made a connection for life.

However, she left my school the next year and went back to her home district. I thought I'd never hear from her again, yet, through the wonderful world of Facebook, we have reconnected years later.

She now has 3 beautiful boys and a wonderful, loving husband. I met them all today. They made me feel as though I were part of their family... and oh! Those precious little boys! Such a blessing!

So, I've been thinking about those students of mine who have touched my life as much as (maybe) I've touched theirs. I have several students who I hold dear and with whom I maintain contact. Yet EVERY student has been a gift to me... I learn something from each one of them, and sometimes, I guess they learn something from me. The fact that they remember me as much as I do them makes me feel so good, so appreciated, so loved.

Seeing my former student today and being able to share mommy stories and give her some of my baby things was such a blessing as well. I'm so proud of her and how beautiful she is from the inside out. She's a woman of great faith, who, in her times of trouble, has never been ashamed to call on the Lord and profess that faith. Now she has a wonderful husband (who I thought was the sweetest thing!) and together they have built a beautiful family. God has blessed her and knows her heart. May she, her husband and her boys continue to be blessed. My hope is, if this actually becomes a real book, I can give her a signed copy.

My prayer today is this:

I thank you, Lord, for all you have given me; from my career, students and colleagues to my family and church family. Please bless everyone I have a chance to share my life with and may we all be together again forever in your kingdom.

In Jesus' name I pray,

Amen

Chill, I've Got This... (Said God, Not Me)

"Be still and know that I am God." Psalm 46:10

Let's be honest, life's a lot sometimes. Between the to-do lists, the mental load, the emotional rollercoasters, and the endless tabs open in my brain (seriously, I think I've got like 43 running at once), it's no wonder we get overwhelmed.

Overthinking, much? Don't even get me started. It's like my brain decides to hold a full-blown committee meeting at 2 a.m. to go over every possible worst-case scenario. Sound familiar?

In a world that practically hands out trophies for being busy, it's easy to feel like we've got to do it all ourselves. Like if we don't hold it together, everything's going to fall apart. But here's the thing, spoiler alert: it's not all on us.

God isn't sitting up in heaven with a checklist, waiting to see if we'll manage it all perfectly before He steps in. He's already there. Already in it. Already working. Even when we're stressed out, freaking out, or completely tapped out. Sometimes I forget that. I get caught up in the chaos and forget to just breathe and remember who's actually in control. Not me. Not my perfectly color-coded planner. Not my high-functioning anxiety disguised as "being on top of things." Nope. God.

Relying on Him doesn't mean we sit around doing nothing, it means we stop trying to carry the whole world on our own shoulders. It means saying, "Okay, God. I'm handing this over to You." And what do we get in exchange? Peace. Not the temporary kind, but the kind that settles your heart even when nothing around you has changed.

I've started thinking of it like a divine trade-in: my stress, my panic, my endless spiral of "what ifs" ... for His calm, steady presence. Not a bad deal. No receipt needed!

Let's be real, God's timing? Yeah, it's rarely what I want, but it's always what I need. I may want answers now (yesterday, preferably), but He sees the whole picture. He's already down the road, making a way. So, I can breathe. I can wait.

I can rest knowing that He hasn't forgotten me.

Not for a second.

So next time everything feels like too much and - trust me, there will be a next time, pause. Take a deep breath. Remind yourself: "God's got this." You're not meant to carry it all. You were never supposed to.

Leaning on Him isn't weakness – it's wisdom. It's peace. It's freedom.

Here's a little prayer for when you're spiraling:

Dear God,

You see the chaos in my heart and the thousand tabs open in my head. Thank You for being patient with me. Help me to breathe, slow down, and hand it all over to You. I'm tired of trying to control everything. I trust that You've got this—even when I don't. Fill me with Your peace and remind me that I'm never, ever alone.

Amen.

You know you have daughters when...

... the last pair of shoes you bought were tap or ballet shoes

... you can't find your new lip gloss, but when you do, it's in your 12-year-old's backpack

... you do more laundry in a week for them than for the adults (and they wear uniforms to school!)

... you wish your 12-year-old would just hurry up and skip over the impending puberty stage because: B*!$#

... you spend more time at the dance studio than you do at home

... you spend more money at the dance studio than you do for your home

... you won't let your daughters wear anything you wore in the 80s; it's "inappropriate" (except when they have 80s Day at school, then your inner Madonna comes out and you make sure your kid looks better than everyone else decked out in 80s style from hair to bobby socks and heels - do NOT judge me!)

... the dog comes out of the girls' bedroom wearing Build-a-Bear clothes from time to time

... you can't go shopping alone anymore (you now have shopping buddies... FOREVER)

... every piece of plastic or wood that you think is garbage ends up in your girls' room because "it can be used for a craft" or "it makes a good ___"

... your 6-year-old grows up FAR quicker than your 12-year-old did, and you don't like it one bit

... your girls' room becomes a disco at times, complete with loud music and crazy lights, you hear giggles and singing, and it makes you smile (mainly because they're getting along for a little while and they're cranking up your favorite 90s dance jams)

... doing your nails means doing THEIR nails, too

... your new hair accessories become THEIR new hair accessories and are now stored in THEIR room

... you always have someone to ask if your outfit/hair looks alright... and they'll be honest, but you won't get angry when they're little. When they become adults? Just don't ask, the same honesty comes out and it might not be kind (you'll be sad)

... you have someone to watch sappy movies with

... you find yourself borrowing one of their nail polishes because they have cool colors and last, but not least:

Finally, you know you have daughters when...

... you have an abundance of "I love Mom" crafts... and you keep every one of them in your heart... and on the refrigerator.

I love you, too, girls... and I wouldn't trade a single moment... but dang, you're expensive!

God bless you all of your days!

> *"Behold, children are a heritage from the Lord, the fruit of the womb a reward."* Psalm 127:3

God's plan in God's time

"Trust in the LORD with all your heart, and do not lean on your own understanding, in all your ways acknowledge him, and he will make straight your paths." Proverbs 3:5-6

"Make me to know your ways, O Lord; teach me your paths. Lead me in your truth and teach me, for you are the God of my salvation; for you I wait all the day long." Psalm 25:4-5

Fate? Karma? (Just stop with those words...ew) Everything happens for a reason, right? We've heard them all... the real reason? Ever wonder why, some days, you seem to catch every red light as you drive somewhere? Ever have a near-miss on the highway as a car veers into another lane without seeing you or others? Ever miss a train? You were meant to... (See chapter: Detours, Distractions, and Divine Grace)

We all have trials in our lives. What is important is that we recognize that God has a plan that was laid out long before and we need to trust Him.

Yes, there will be heartache, tragedy and illness; "lean not on your own understanding" and trust in the Lord. There is a reason why everything happens, though we may never know or understand why.

God has a plan for you.

My girls and I started going to Emanuel back in 2009. That time of my life there was a lot of change and a lot of challenge. My personal relationships were tensed, my faith was shaken, and I felt as though I had hit rock bottom in life. That year I lost 80 lbs., discovered my new church home, and did some deep soul-searching and cleansing as I turned 40. What a journey that had been!

I now know, since then, that everything that I went through was part of God's plan for me. I never would be able to be where I am today (emotionally or spiritually) without experiencing everything that God put in my path. I will forever trust in God's will for my life. For I know that, though bumpy at times, my paths will be straight!

Dear Lord, I thank you for the comfort of knowing that You are in control. Please continue to be with me and help me to always trust you, honor Your plan for me and Submit to You so my paths may be straight.

In Jesus' name,

Amen

Psalm 46

"God is our refuge and strength, a very present help in trouble." Psalm 46:1

We all need comfort from time to time. We all experience pain, heartache, disappointment, worry, anxiety, and fear. Sometimes we forget the promise of an eternal, beautiful, pain-free life in Heaven. God promises He is with us every day in every way. He knows our innermost thoughts. He knows when we are troubled. He is not only there by us, He's gone ahead and knows your path.

Psalm 46 is a promise of His big, loving arms wrapped around us, loving us, shielding us from hurt, in a most incredible embrace! As a parent, I know the feeling of wanting to protect my children from anything that gives them pain, sadness, fear, anxiety, and worry. The best way I can do that is not just with MY love, support, protection, and hugs, but to constantly remind my girls of their Heavenly Father's forever promise in His Word.

"God is in the midst of her; she shall not be moved;" Psalm 46:5

So, I will ask in prayer for help to live a life in demonstration of my trust and faith in His comfort. I do this and pray that my children and others around me may see His work within me and that this may help them to grow in faith and closeness to Him.

My little gift to my children today is going to be a little card with Psalm 46 that I'll write in prayerful meditation. I invite

346

you to do the same for someone you know can use the comfort of our omnipresent Father.

Psalm 46

God is our refuge and strength,
*   a very present help in trouble.*
Therefore, we will not fear though the earth gives way,
*   though the mountains be moved into the heart of the sea,*
though its waters roar and foam,
*   though the mountains tremble at its swelling. Selah*

There is a river whose streams make glad the city of God,
*   the holy habitation of the Most High.*
God is in the midst of her; she shall not be moved;
*   God will help her when morning dawns.*
The nations rage, the kingdoms totter;
*   he utters his voice, the earth melts.*
The Lord of hosts is with us;
*   the God of Jacob is our fortress. Selah*

Come, behold the works of the Lord,
*   how he has brought desolations on the earth.*
He makes wars cease to the end of the earth;
*   he breaks the bow and shatters the spear;*
*   he burns the chariots with fire.*
"Be still, and know that I am God.
*   I will be exalted among the nations,*
*   I will be exalted in the earth!"*
The Lord of hosts is with us;
*   the God of Jacob is our fortress.*

Word of God Speak

Do a web search for the video of this amazing song by MercyMe. The chorus says,

> *"To be still and know that you're in this place, please let me stay and rest in your holiness...Word of God, speak."*

Too often I deny myself the time to sit and just BE. It's then when I fall into traps: I worry, I eat, I spend money I shouldn't, I say things that are dumb. I need to retrain my brain to focus on Him leading me only. I have to learn to let Him calm the tumultuous waters of my life! I need to be in His Presence and let Him take over my thoughts, my heart, my entire existence.

He's got this.

> *"Yet I am always with you; you*
> *hold me by my right hand.*
> *You guide me with your counsel, and*
> *afterward you will take me into glory.*
> *Whom have I in heaven but you?*
> *And earth has nothing I desire besides you.*
> *My flesh and my heart may fail,*
> *but God is the strength of my heart*
> *and my portion forever." Psalm 73:23-26*

It's possibly one of the most difficult things to do, but I will try to stop myself from freaking out, overthinking and succumbing to compulsive behaviors. Yes, that's human nature, but, hey,

"I can do all things through him who strengthens me."
Philippians 4:13

Take a moment to be still. When things are crazy, stop, sit somewhere quiet, talk to Your Father. He's right there waiting to hear from you. Let Him take care of it; He's got this!

Be blessed in His Presence!'

(and go check out that MercyMe video)

Omniscient – Omnipotent – Omnipresent

(aka. God knows everything, can do anything, and is literally everywhere... so maybe don't try to hide.)

Let's break this down.

God is omniscient (He knows everything), omnipotent (He can do anything), and omnipresent (He is everywhere, all the time).

Sounds a little intimidating, right? I mean, that's a whole lot of power, presence, and awareness. And yes—if your faith is on shaky ground or if you're in a season of running away from God (been there, done that), those words might sound more like a warning label than a warm hug.

Let's pause for a second and look again:

> *"the Lord—knows the thoughts of man, that they are but a breath"* Psalm 94:11

> *"so that all the peoples of the earth may know that the hand of the Lord is mighty, that you may fear the Lord your God forever."* Joshua 4:24

> *"Am I a God at hand, declares the Lord, and not a God far away? Can a man hide himself in secret places so that I cannot see him? declares the Lord. Do I not fill heaven and earth? declares the Lord."* Jeremiah 23:23–24

At first glance, these verses might seem like they're written in bold, red, warning-font. However, if you dig a little deeper, you'll find something much more comforting hiding underneath all that holy power: reassurance.

Let's be honest—we're a mess.

We sin, constantly. We say things we shouldn't. We don't say the things we should. We hurt people unintentionally, and sometimes intentionally! We have pride, bitterness, fear, selfishness... half the time we don't even know the full extent of our own junk.

Hey, guess what? God does.

He sees all of it. The spoken and the silent. The mess and the motive. The surface and the soul. And yet...

He still chooses to love us. He still listens when we pray. He still offers grace when we confess. He still forgives us, even for the stuff we didn't realize we needed forgiveness for.

Think about that for a second. The all-knowing, all-powerful, all-present God isn't waiting to zap us when we mess up. He's waiting for us to come to Him so He can clean us up— *with mercy, with grace, with a love that doesn't flinch.*

> *"Most merciful God, we confess that we are by nature sinful and unclean. We have sinned against You in thought, word, and deed, by what we have done and by what we have left undone..."*
>
> —from the Lutheran confession of sins

He knows it all.

Still, He invites us in.

So no, you can't hide from Him. Why would you want to?

There's nothing more freeing than being fully known, and still fully loved. That's what makes His omniscience, omnipotence, and omnipresence not scary, but sacred.

Lord God,

You are all-knowing, all-powerful, and always present— and yet, You are gentle, merciful, and full of grace. Thank You for seeing every part of me— even the pieces I try to ignore or hide— and choosing to love me anyway. Forgive me for the things I've done, and for the things I've left undone. For the words I've spoken in haste, and the truths I've been too afraid to say. You know them all, and still, You call me Yours. Help me not to fear Your all-seeing eyes, but to rest in the comfort of Your constant presence.

When I wander, bring me back. When I fail, lift me up. When I forget, remind me— Your grace is greater than my mess. Thank You for loving me as I am, and for shaping me into who You've created me to be.

In Jesus' holy and powerful name,

Amen.

Mid-week Worship

We have a different type of worship service at my church on Wednesday evenings; a mid-week "freshen-up" if you will. We begin with some praise music that is awesome and uplifting. We open with prayer and sing some more. Then usually an elder or two and other lay leaders give a message, lesson, or testimony.

Sometimes we do a guided Bible study for a few weeks, or we might even watch episodes of The Chosen. The evening finishes with a prayer with personal petitions of thanksgiving or for healing and God's constant blessing, then one more awesome praise song to wrap it all up.

Each week presents a new theme. One week, the theme was "How Do You Get Your Worship On?" and I was asked to give testimony. So, there I sat, inspired and called to write, and mentally preparing for later. I guess I'll share here what I said that night!

A devotion I read that morning said "Worship is more than a Sunday morning duty. It is a daily loving response to our mighty and loving God." Perfectly stated. When I thought about how I get my worship on, I didn't automatically think about Sunday morning; I worship constantly (well, I try, ok?).

Do I need to be in church at all? Do I need to be with other people? Not necessarily (but it's definitely cool). Look, we all went through the Covid mess and did NOT get to be together in person for a while. Anyway, here's what the dictionary says about what worship is:

worship (n.) the feeling or expression of reverence and adoration for a deity (v.) to show reverence and adoration for a deity

So, referring to my chapter asking, "Who's Your Daddy?", we have to remember that if our thoughts are not on God or on what's righteous and holy, we are tempted to make gods out of those other things (like worries, fears, anxiety, your job, money issues, Amazon, even your cell phone!) and worship them instead! When we are clearly instructed in the first Commandment that we are to have no other gods.

> *"for you shall worship no other god, for the Lord, whose name is Jealous, is a jealous God."* Exodus 34:14

> *"You shall love the Lord your God with all your heart and with all your soul and with all your might"* Deuteronomy 6:5

Therefore, we pray and ask for our thoughts to be brought back to Him. Something like this might do the trick:

Lord, my thoughts and focus are wandering. Help me get back on track and put You first. I ask this is Jesus' name. Amen

So tonight, I'm going to talk about how I worship: *music, prayer, devotion, writing, thoughts.* Those aren't in any particular order, but I'll address them as such.

Music: I was raised in a traditional, liturgical Missouri Synod Lutheran church. Back when I was a kid, we used the "TLH" (The Lutheran Hymnal) and, from a young age, I had pretty much everything from p. 5 forward memorized. (I still enjoy singing it and am rather proud that I still remember it!) As a teen when I joined the choir I learned my "part" (as a music geek, this was cool...altos of the LCMS unite!).

Growing up in a musical family, and raising my girls the same, music in our church service is incredibly important. However, music is a part of my life from the time I wake in the morning and EVERY.DAY.

Sunday mornings I discovered the radio show "Religion and Rock" on one of my favorite rock stations. It's hosted by Monsignor Jim Vlaun, a RC priest who plays a great collection of rock songs and ties each into a message about righteous living in Christ. Awesome show. He has some cool insight and helps me get my mind straight for my coming worship (I show him a bit of grace for being RC - Lol).

Wednesday evening worship is a great place for me to reconnect with God through music and a message. I love to hear our favorites and some even take me into a special place with Him where I can focus on Him only. (Check out the song "Agnus Dei" by Michael W. Smith... *chills*)

Contemporary Christian music is a big deal these days. I have a few songs in a playlist that really resonate with my soul, and The Message on SiriusXM is locked in on preset in my car. I'd love to get more into this. It's a matter of committing to listening and abandoning my beloved rock or hip-hop stations for a while. Stay tuned. (Check out "Look Up, Child" by Lauren Daigle... I listen to that one on a loop.)

Prayer: I have started to pray from the time I open my eyes in the morning until I lay my head on the pillow at night. I start and end my day talking to God. I pray with my daughter in the car. I pray when I see certain buildings or landmarks as I drive because I am reminded of His incomprehensible creation. I pray during my breaks at work. I pray at meals, in restaurants, and before important events (like my daughters' recitals, concerts and competitions). I never "hang up the call", I just keep talking.

Devotion: I've been reading Jesus Calling by Sarah Young everyday with my first cup of coffee. My youngest also has the Jesus Calling for Kids app for iOS. We read it together in the morning before we leave and it sets our minds on a good path, giving us something to discuss and think about throughout the day. I also get a devotion emailed to me each day but read it usually later in the day. Of course, I couldn't get by without my brothers and sisters in Christ to provide me with verses, devotions and words of encouragement.

Writing: I've tried the blog thing a few times. I tend to have spurts of big writing, then lulls of nothing. It started a few years ago when I wrote devotions for my church's Lenten Devotional.

I caught the writing bug and have dabbled ever since. Let's see how long I can keep this book thing going. (I'm guessing if you're reading this, then it did.) It's a way for me to keep my thoughts on my faith.

Thoughts: I worship God in my thoughts all day long. I'm a sinner by nature, as we all are, but I do my best to refocus and keep my heart full of Him and filled with the Holy Spirit. The other day, as my youngest and I were reading our devotion, this is what Jesus told us:

"Today, let your goal be to capture every thought and bring it to Me. Wherever your mind wanders, lasso those thoughts and show them to Me. Having anxious thoughts? They shrivel up and disappear when My Light shines on them. Having confused thoughts? My Peace will come untangle them. Starting to think you're better than someone else? My unconditional Love will help you see that I love all My children, and so should you. Keep your thoughts focused on Me so that you can enjoy My Peace." - Jesus Calling

Tonight, at mid-week worship, I hope to share my personal ways to "get my worship on" so others may be blessed and grow in their faith. When I choose to worship God all day long, I am pleasing in His sight and He blesses me beyond explanation and comprehension.

Be blessed. Peace.

Above All

"Crucified, laid behind a stone;
You lived to die, rejected and alone;
Like a rose, trampled on the ground,
You took the fall, and thought of me... above all"

Of all the hymns and praise songs we sing, "Above All" is the one that brings me to tears the most. I can't say that each tear is a sad one; most of my tears are happy ones!

Lent is a season of contemplation and meditation. We read the Gospel accounts of the 40 days before Christ hung on the cross, died and rose triumphant over sin. Sadness prevails during these weeks, evident by silencing our alleluias until Easter morning.

Yet we can take comfort in the reward! While never fully dismissing the horror of Christ's death, we must focus on the resurrection, our deliverance from our sinful life with the promise of heavenly life!

So, when I sing that verse to the song "Above All," I am reminded not only of the torture and abuse of Jesus, but of His immense, unconditional love for sinful, unworthy ME! During Lent, where Christ's death brings so much sadness, His rising on that Easter morning brings great joy!

Never lose sight of that.

Pray with me...

Heavenly Father,

You sent Your Son to deliver us from eternal damnation because we are inherently sinful. Your mercy on us is unimaginable! We thank you for your immeasurable love and ask that You send Your Holy Spirit to us so we may remember Christ's ultimate sacrifice... because for our sins, He took the fall, and thought of us, above all.

In Jesus' precious name,

Amen

Jesus NEVER Fails You, He'll NEVER Let You Down

Has anyone ever let you down? Disappointed you? I find myself so deeply saddened when this happens. I am cut to the bone. I obsess over words spoken; I have recurring nightmares about past actions. It consumes me, lives rent free in my brain, and I am broken.

He wasn't supposed to act like that!

She wasn't supposed to hurt me, she loves me!

Why does he do this to me?

How could she talk to me that way?

After many years of being let down, emotionally beat down even, I am learning to recognize when it happens.

So, now what? With my ability to acknowledge when others are hurting me, what's my next step? I can choose how I'm going to cope. I go to Jesus.

I used to stay down for a long time. I couldn't get up. Knowing when it's happening now, I can go to the Word. I can let Jesus give me His outstretched hand; I will take it and allow Him to lift me up. When I seek His presence, He calms me. When I ask for His comfort, He blesses me.

So, WHY is it so d@mn difficult to LET HIM IN?

Recently I tried to pray but I couldn't even get words out in coherent sentences because I fell so hard. God led me to make a word cloud that I used to give Him my prayer (if you've never heard of a word cloud, do a web search... there are free programs and it's super fun; I used wordart.com for the one below). All I did was input words of what I needed and wanted, picked some cool colors, and refreshed the page until I liked how the words were aligned. Not only did it come out pretty cool, it worked.

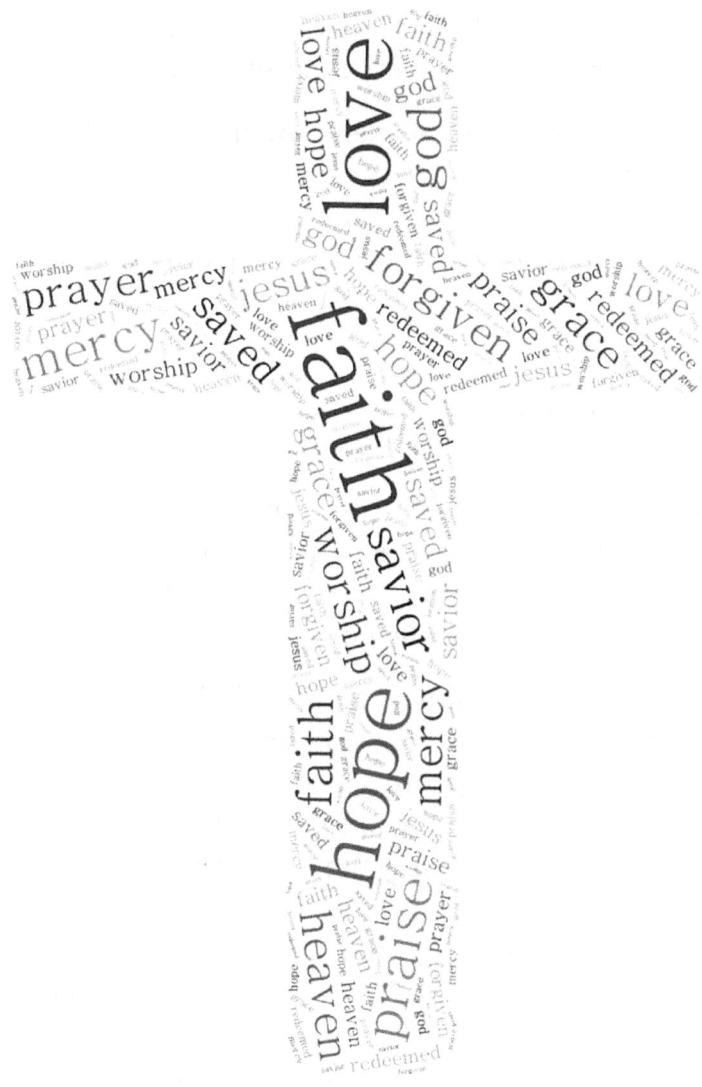

Love

I can't imagine not feeling love.

There are, from what I've learned in Bible studies, three types of love: eros, philos and agape, each are translated as "love" in English, but they all mean very different things in Greek.

Eros love is physical, in a sense. It might be one of the easiest loves to feel. I guess it's the kind of "love" that is expressed when someone talks about "loving" movie stars or athletes. Famous people who are aesthetically pleasing and are often lusted after with eros. It's also the love that makes us romantically attracted to our spouses.

> *"Let him kiss me with the kisses of his mouth - for your love is better than wine."* Song of Solomon 1:2

The Song of Solomon celebrates eros — physical attraction within the sanctity of marriage — as a beautiful gift from God. *Eros* has a holy place within marriage, and this verse affirms its sacredness. I get that. I feel it.

Philos is different altogether. It's the kind of love that I have for my family, my friends, my coworkers, and my neighbors. True friendship (philos) is revealed in kindness and loyalty. I will be there to support, encourage, and comfort them. Like the city Philadelphia meaning the "City of Brotherly Love," it's a compassionate love that I feel when I am respected and treated with kindness and respect. When people I see at work wish me a happy Mother's Day the Friday before that weekend, I feel it. When they ask how my Christmas was, I feel it. When they wish me a happy birthday, I feel it.

"A friend loves at all times, and a brother is born for a time of adversity." Proverbs 17:17

I have *philos* for my husband, too. What kind of marriage could we have without philos? He is my friend, we started as friends, he will always be my friend...A marriage rooted in friendship is strong — lifting each other up in partnership and love... and I feel it.

"Two are better than one, because they have a good reward for their toil. For if they fall, one will lift up his fellow. But woe to him who is alone when he falls and has not another to lift him up!" Ecclesiastes 4:9–10

Agape is that ultimate, spiritual love that is best exemplified by God's love for us. He loves me so much that I am forgiven, washed clean in the blood of His Son who He sacrificed for ME. I am a "poor, miserable sinner" and I will never be able to stop no matter how hard I try. So, my only out is to own up to my sins, the ones I know about and the ones I'm clueless about. HE knows them all and He is STILL willing to forgive me when I seek Him and ask for His mercy and grace. Amazing... I feel it.

"but God shows his love for us in that while we were still sinners, Christ died for us." Romans 5:8

This is the ultimate verse for explaining agape: sacrificial love given freely, even when we don't deserve it (grace). By contrast, He does NOT give us what we DO deserve, and that's the definition of "mercy".

"The steadfast love of the Lord never ceases; his mercies never come to an end; they are new every

morning; great is your faithfulness" Lamentations 3:22–23

Agape is also what I have for MY children. I don't think I can accurately describe my love for them. I loved them before I knew them. No matter what they do or who they become, I will love them. The internet definition of *Agape:*

> *a selfless, unconditional love, a love that acts regardless of circumstances or feelings. It is a love that gives, serves, and sacrifices for the well-being of the loved one*

I feel it...forever.

> *"As one whom his mother comforts, so I will comfort you; you shall be comforted in Jerusalem."* Isaiah 66:13

Little hands wrapped around my neck, special pictures scribbled on a napkin at a restaurant that I'm supposed to keep forever, flowers (weeds) from the lawn handed to me that I have to put into a glass of water on my kitchen windowsill... they love me (agape).

My girls show me a love that nothing else compares to; a love that will never end or tarnish. THIS is the love that God has for US! After all, we are His children!

And I feel it.

So, in essence, the love we feel is so complex because it comes in many forms: physical, mental and spiritual. What's so unbelievable to me is how I have love to give in all forms...and I feel it.

Epilogue

For the Sister Who Still Feels "Slappy"

Look at you. You made it all the way to the end — not just of this book, but of something bigger. A mindset. A moment. A version of you that maybe needed to be laid down so something new could rise up.

I'm proud of you. No really — I am. Because showing up to a workbook about how to be a Christian woman when you still want to slap people? That takes honesty. That takes humility. That takes a woman who knows she needs Jesus and a little bit of caffeine to get through most days.

If you laughed at "Life as a Type-A," cried through "The One That Wandered," shouted "Amen!" during "Why I Do What I Do," or underlined every other sentence in "Cast Me Not Away" — then you and I are already kindred spirits.

You get it.

You get grace.

You get that faith isn't a Pinterest board or a spiritual to-do list. It's showing up — in the mess, in the hard, in the Target parking lot when someone steals your spot and you have to call on the name of the Lord and quickly.

What now? It's not the end just because you finished the book. Let it be the beginning of the next part of your journey. Maybe start a small group; gather a few friends and walk through this again, together. Pick a book of the Bible and journal about it using the format from this book.

At minimum, get yourself a nice notebook and start writing daily asking yourself, "Where did I see God today?"

Here's what I hope you take with you: You are not a project. You are not behind. You are not the exception to God's promises. You are seen, loved, called, forgiven, and still being transformed. Every stumble is still part of your story. Every prayer, even the desperate, ugly ones, is heard. And every step forward — even the tiniest, wobbly, mustard-seed step — is a victory.

So, go. Be salty (Matthew 5:13). Stay lit (Matthew 5:14). Let grace fuel your fire. And when the world feels too loud and your patience feels paper-thin, remember: You are not alone. God is with you, cheering you on — and so am I.

May your coffee be strong, your prayers be bolder, and your faith be rooted deeper than ever before. You're His, sister.

Always have been.

Always will be.

Peace and love to you always!

Your sassy, snarky, flawed and forgiven sister,

Kim

Acknowledgements

Each of these people have a part in this book somehow

Eric: for being there when I'm cranky and still loving me and supporting me as I am; none of this would be possible without you, your love, support, humor, and grace

Sara and Bela: for changing my life forever (for the better); I love you more than I will ever be able to express

Mom and Dad: for putting up with my crap and still loving me through it all

Aunt Sue: for always keeping me in your prayers and constantly providing me with Christian guidance and support as my Godmother

Aunt Peg: for the lemon merengue pie recipe that will live on forever; for ceramics, Barry Manilow, and my cousins... I will treasure your memory in my heart forever

Nicole Bevers: for being my first friend, my forever friend... I miss you more than I can express

Elissa Zadrozny: for coming into my life just when I needed you, first in the 80s and again in the 2020s... don't go anywhere, ok?

Michele: for letting me vent and making me laugh when I've wanted to cry; Lerk! I wrert a berk!... love you, bestie

Deb: for being REAL and creating our little friend group

Harry: for getting my faith back on track; I wouldn't be where I am today without you

Ladies Who Lunch: for being the ones I know I can count on, I love you all

Nancy Barrett: for encouraging me when we worked on the devotional and beyond

Honey Pabst: for being there when it all started (my first Sunday School teacher) and now my LWML mentor

Laura Riggio: for SO MANY good talks and all your awesome advice (and dog-sitting)

Ann Carney: for being my country b!#$ and teaching me to let loose and enjoy life

Jimmy Davis: for sharing daily devotions, your awesome faith, friendship, and sense of humor

Pastor Steve: for arriving in my life just when I was ready for making the next step in my faith journey; your support and encouragement are such a blessing

Natalie: for being part of the decision process for your coming to Emanuel, being a friend to me and to Sara, being a Master Thrifter, and just being your fun, lovable self!

Former students: Liz, Sara, Katherine, Sarah, Ann, Anthony, Shannon, geez, there are just SO MANY of you in my heart: I love each and every one of you as though you were my own children and you each have given me a gift that has made me who I am today (the good stuff I promise)

My Godchildren Casey, Ethen and Shane: for allowing me the honor being your Godmother, even though I fall short

Diann DeJulia: for teaching me algebra, the love of factoring polynomials, and the value of a longtime, long-distance friendship... oh, and for making me belly laugh since 1984

Tara Hill: for being my burning bush; imagine that, shilly goosh

Hilary Porter: for keeping it real in OG... I'm more me with you when I'm there

Jean Roth: for being in my life when I was so lost, you helped me so much; when I join you in Heaven, let's lie on our backs, look at something beautiful, ponder His gifts, and praise Him; do-bee-do-bee-do

Deaconess Rojas: for being such an inspiration as a woman in ministry

Jon Ellingworth (and Lisa!): for being there when I finally "got it", for being an amazing shepherd to me all these years (whether you knew you were or not), and for inspiring me to write through my journey

Martin Luther: for being so bold in the Lord to change how so many walk in their faith, for allowing me to celebrate Reformation Day by posting amazing Luther memes and giving me a better reason for celebrating October 31... you rock, my dude!

Ocean Grove, NJ: for changing my faith beyond what I could have ever imagined, for the friends I have there and the life I love to live; and I get to have all of that by the ocean! You are My Happy Place!

Check out:

www.favordeipress.com

for free, printable journal pages,

news of upcoming books,

and to contact me for

signings and speaking events

www.ingramcontent.com/pod-product-compliance
Lightning Source LLC
Chambersburg PA
CBHW061552120626
46550CB00004B/1453